Your Roaring Twenties

Avoid the Paycheck-to-Paycheck
Life as a Twentysomething

MATT MORRILL

First e-book edition: June 2015

ISBN-13: 978-1512360981

ISBN-10: 1512360988

This book is dedicated to my mother and father, both of whom taught me the value of a dollar.

CONTENTS

ACKNOWLEDGMENTS

I heard somewhere that you should only write a book if you have something to say. Thankfully, my friends and family never disowned me when I brought up the topic of personal finance for the millionth time in conversation. I want to thank my mother and father for instilling thriftiness in me from a young age. I want to also thank my close friends— conversations with them were the inspiration for this book. Special thanks to my Mom and Martha Talley for providing copyediting support. My partner, Emily, also provided editing support throughout. I'm grateful to her for so much more beyond this book. Finally, this book is also dedicated to my little brother. I'm sure by now he's probably sick of my advice, but I hope he is able to learn some tricks from reading this.

INTRODUCTION

Invest in Your Financial Education

"An investment in knowledge always pays the best interest." –
Benjamin Franklin

It's amazing some of the small things you remember from
high school and college. Though it's been over ten years, I
still remember what the Wilmot Proviso was from AP US
History, and I could also run you through the basics of
photosynthesis from biology. I still recall the names of
different periods of American architecture, like neoclassicism
and Greek Revival, and I could spout off the Pythagorean
theorem to you if I gave it some thought. One thing I don't
remember from school is learning how to manage credit
cards. I don't recollect lessons on how a loan works, and I
really don't recall doing homework on the differences
between stocks and bonds. I definitely don't remember any
lessons about the power of inflation.

The reason I don't remember these is because they were
never covered in my courses. It's a cruel twist that most of
the knowledge we learn throughout high school and college is

seldom used while the know-how we actually need is not formally taught, forcing us to learn through self-education and trial and error. This lack of financial literacy is costing us billions of dollars annually. Most worrisome of all, though, are the bad decisions this lack of education is causing. People take on hundreds of thousands in debt for a degree that may never earn them above the median household income of $52,000. They rack up thousands of dollars in credit card debt without fully understanding the consequences of doing so. They buy new, expensive luxury cars but don't invest any money in retirement savings. Few have sufficient emergency savings to cover six months' worth of expenses in the event of a job loss or other catastrophe. As many life events like marriage and having children happen at older and older ages, these bad decisions are becoming especially problematic for the millennial generation. Some are arriving at age 30 with financial circumstances little different from when they were 20.

This book is in part a response to the multitude of stories out there involving people in their 20s and 30s who are swimming in debt with limited employment prospects. These are stories like Danielle Owens's. Owens graduated from Georgetown Law in 2010, and despite applying for hundreds of jobs, found herself jobless with $200,000 in debt, forcing her to go on welfare. They're stories like that of Michelle Holshue, who despite graduating with a degree in nursing clips coupons so she can make payments on her $140,000 in student loans. Some don't even have savings accounts, and for those who do, a large portion have less than $5,000 saved. For many older millennials, reality is just not living up to expectations, and major decisions like having kids and buying a house are pushed further down the road because they're just not feasible in the present.

Consider your own situation for a second as you sit reading this. Now, fast-forward 40 years into the future. What kind of life do you envision? For many people, 65 and beyond is envisaged as a time of relaxation, free of worries about money and work. A house paid off (and maybe a vacation home, too), kids' college tuition already paid, and a hefty nest egg to support you as you enjoy your golden years. This will not be the reality for most people. The median net worth for those approaching retirement is nowhere near what is needed to support a comfortable life. Though Social Security and Medicare benefits exist now, they pay a pittance, and they may not be around forever. The saddest part is that for people approaching retirement, the book has already been written: there is little they can do to avert poverty for the remainder of their lives if they haven't saved enough.

If you're still in your twenties and early thirties, the good news is that you can still write your own future. Unlike those approaching retirement, you have a critical supply of the ultimate precious resource: time. As you'll see in this book, actions you take early on resonate and amplify throughout the years so that small steps taken now can pay big dividends (or cause huge hardships) later.

Think about where you want to be in 40 years, then work backwards from that point. What does your life look like in your 50s? How about your 40s and 30s? Do you feel you're on the path to realize this vision? If you're feeling a bit insecure about your prospects, keep reading. Personal finance class is in session.

How to Get Smart on Personal Finance

The first stop on the road to securing your future is

investing in your financial education. This truly is an investment: you will need to spend significant time learning the basics of personal finance and economics, especially if you did not get much exposure to these areas in college. Think about how much time people spend studying for their SAT, ACT, LSAT, GMAT, GRE and other acronym tests – in many cases, this can amount to hundreds of hours. Now, by comparison, think about how much time an average person deliberately invests in becoming financially literate: it's usually a mere fraction of their standardized test work, if at all. There's one other big difference, too. While knowing how to solve a complex SAT math problem or GMAT data sufficiency question probably won't be much use after you take the test, lessons you learn in your quest for financial literacy will pay huge returns throughout your lifetime. It doesn't take an aspiring MBA student to tell you which is the better deal.

Personally, I was a history major who didn't take a single business or finance class while in college. Though I had always been a saver, I realized pretty quickly after graduation that I needed to learn the basics of personal finance to reach my life goals. I'm the poster child of someone who needed financial education. Fortunately, I recognized this dearth of knowledge early on and made learning personal finance a major life priority. The resources I used to do this fell into a few broad categories:

Websites and Blogs: One of the best ways to begin your financial education is by following a blog or website that is both interesting and educational. These are also great because you can search for specific questions ("how does a mortgage work?") and get answers from multiple different viewpoints. I've found www.getrichslowly.org to be particularly useful, and I regularly read the Financial Samurai blog. For those interested in frugal living, there is a whole sub-culture around optimizing your expenses to retire early as seen through blogs like Frugal Woods and Mr. Money Moustache.

Podcasts: You're crammed into a subway train or bus, stuck against other sweaty passengers, and it's a good 30 minutes until the next time you experience fresh air. Might as well learn about some personal finance during your commute! While episodes of *Comedy Bang! Bang!* and *The Adam Corolla Show* are hilarious, they probably aren't doing a ton for your brain. Instead, look into podcasts like American Public Media's *Marketplace Money,* NPR's *Planet Money,* and others like *Stuff Mom Never Told You, Stacking Benjamins,* and *Listen, Money Matters!* These are all great ways to passively graze on financial knowledge and pick up tips through osmosis.

Books: Finally, yes, it's a fine idea to pick up a good old-fashioned book every now and then, though I'd also include eBooks in this category, of course. There are a plethora of books I've found useful in my own journey, and not all of them have been directly related to finance. While books like Dave Ramsey's *Total Money Makeover,* Robert Kiyosaki's *Rich Dad, Poor Dad,* and Jeff Rose's *Soldier of Finance* all helped me understand the basic principles of personal finance, others like Meg Jay's *The Defining Decade,* Carol Dweck's *Mindset,* Dale Carnegie's *How to Win Friends and Influence People*, and Stephen Covey's *7 Habits of Highly Effective People* have all taught me invaluable lessons on how to create a strategic roadmap for my life.

Experience: The mother of all teachers can be a harsh one, but sometimes there's no better way to learn how something works than through trial and error. For instance, it's hard to imagine how a 401K works until you actually have one for retirement savings, and it's difficult to comprehend the benefits of passive income until you've invested in some bonds or real estate. Your parents can be crucial resources to you due to their experience, but remember to apply the same scrutiny to their advice as you would to the advice of others – it's important to avoid your parents' mistakes if possible. Experience also serves as a motivator: unlike school, in which you may learn theories that you never apply in real life, the theories and strategies learned in personal finance are immediately applicable to real-world situations. Thus, experience begets statements like "I wish I had known x," which serve as powerful motivators for further learning.

If you want to be financially secure, you need to take your financial education seriously. Of course, your own approach does not have to follow the above path, and each person's journey will be slightly different. As opposed to the type of learning you might do to pass a test or get a good grade, think of your financial education as something that is accretive. No one learns everything the first time around, and it takes many years of education to chart a proper course.

Despite all of the advice and strategies available in the resources above, some people might think that it's already too late for them. You may be thinking that you're a spender, and that's how you'll always be. Maybe you've had some setbacks in the stock market and have come to the conclusion that you're just not good at investing, so why bother. Not too long ago, I thought this way, both about segments of my finances and other parts of my life as well. Dr. Carol Dweck's *Mindset* changed that.

Fixed vs. Growth Mindset: Applied to Your Personal Finances

Think about how you view your own progress in life, including all your major wins and setbacks to date. When setbacks occurred, did you divert your efforts away from that area, convinced that it was not worth your time? Or, did you double your effort to push through, enjoying learning something new even if it was via failure? Were your wins "inevitable," in your eyes, or were they a result of hard work and a lot of trial and error?

Dr. Dweck's theory is that there are basically two types of mindsets people have when they look at their lives. In the first "fixed" mindset, people view themselves as a predefined persona with innate skills. People with the fixed mindset believe that they only need to find out what they're meant to do, what they're naturally good at. Anything that is difficult or that results in failure is something that's not worth their effort because it doesn't use their innate skills. Failure is a challenge to their self-worth, and challenging situations can be emotionally devastating under this outlook. The second "growth" mindset is a little different. People with this mindset feel invigorated by challenges and failures because they represent opportunities for growth and improvement. A great example of the contrast between the two mindsets is when you hear people talk about whether they are "math people" or not. People with the fixed mindset will often say "I can't do that, I'm not a math person, so I'm going to stick with what I know." Growth-minded individuals will take on a challenging math problem with gusto, even if they can't solve it. The excitement of learning something new outweighs any damage to their pride and self-worth caused by not solving the problem.

I believe this way of viewing the world can be applied to personal finance. Ask yourself if you're more of a fixed or growth mindset person overall, then take a look at how you approach your finances. If you lost money in the stock market in 2008-2011, did you decide to give up investing for good? Are you a big time spender, and do you think you'll always be that way due to your nature? Do you feel that no matter what decisions you make now, you'll inevitably end up rich and happy? If you answered yes to any of the above, you may have a fixed mindset when it comes to your finances. Why change, since it won't have an effect on anything anyways?

I'd argue that a much more productive mindset to have is the growth mindset. People with the growth mindset don't let setbacks completely derail them. Rather, these setbacks are opportunities for learning, and they might have important clues on what to do differently next time. If people aren't rich at the moment, they see no reason why they can't be rich someday – but they also understand the hard work, challenges, and tradeoffs of pursuing that goal. They also recognize that they have control over their lives. If they spend too much, they can change their habits so that they spend less. Nothing is set in stone.

Your Personal Mission Statement

Another book that I can say changed my life, without exaggeration, is *The 7 Habits of Highly Effective People*. Written by Stephen Covey, the book outlines habits such as being proactive, beginning with the end in mind, and putting first things first. I highly recommend reading the book in its entirety. However, there's one section I found particularly enlightening that focuses on developing your own Personal

Mission Statement.

You're probably familiar with companies that have mission statements. For instance, Vanguard's is "To take a stand for all investors, to treat them fairly, and to give them the best chance for investment success." In addition to its famous "don't be evil" slogan, Google outlines ten principles that sum up its values on its website. Trader Joe's is "to give our customers the best food and beverage values they can find anywhere and to provide them with the information required to make informed buying decisions. We provide these with a dedication to the highest quality of customer satisfaction delivered with a sense of warmth, friendliness, fun, individual pride, and company spirit." The simple phrase is actually extremely important as it boils down the values, goals, and beliefs of the organization into just a few words. Covey suggests that everyone should have a mission statement, not just Fortune 500 companies.

Just as a company can't generate a mission statement in a single afternoon meeting, individuals shouldn't develop their mission statements in the half hour they have before bed. A valuable mission statement takes time to develop and is updated often. A personal mission statement encapsulates your principles, roles, and goals. It can be as simple as a sentence or two or as long as a page. The important part is that it imbues your life with purpose and meaning, without which it is difficult to plan for the future.

Here are just a few examples of personal mission statements:

"To be a teacher. And to be known for inspiring my students to be more than they thought they could be." – Oprah Winfrey

"To serve as a leader, live a balanced life, and apply ethical principles to make a significant difference." – Denise Morrison, CEO of Campbell Soup

"To have fun in my journey through life and learn from my mistakes." – Richard Branson, The Virgin Group

As for myself, I've expanded my personal mission statement into nine principles. I've listed the four most relevant to this book below:

1) I will be a hard worker, maximizing my potential and focusing on the jobs and tasks that fulfill me
2) I will treat money as a means to an end, not an end unto itself; money means security, so my first goal is to secure my future, then my family's future, with it.
3) I will strive to learn something new every day. I will proactively build new skills and knowledge areas
4) I will remember to be thankful for all I have in this world, especially the extremely fortunate starting place I was born into, keeping in mind the difficult situations others grew up in and have faced through no fault of their own

A personal mission statement is your compass and your guide. It points you in a direction and keeps you on that path when you're tempted to diverge from it. Applied to personal finance, it can help keep you honest to yourself when it becomes difficult to do the things that will help you meet your goals. It is very difficult to implement some of the strategies this book suggests without a clear understanding of who you are and where you'd like to go.

Let's Get Started

This book contains six lessons I've learned as I've progressed through my twenties. Though at the time of this writing I'm still a little bit shy of 30, I think that overall I've exceeded my expectations of where I'd be at this point financially. For the record, I don't consider myself an expert: these strategies are based on the research I've conducted and experiences I've had throughout my first several years in the workforce. Mostly, they're based on my desire to share things I did that worked well and warn others against the things I tried that turned out poorly. Here are the recommendations outlined in this book:

1. Invest in Your Financial Education
2. Save More, Spend Less
3. Never Live Alone
4. You're Not Smarter Than Mr. Market
5. Find a Job You Don't Hate
6. Think Long and Hard About Grad School

The great news is we've already learned the first lesson, which is to Invest in Your Financial Education! This step is critical as it determines your success in implementing the strategies that follow. We'll next discuss why saving and cost optimization are so critical to your success, after which we'll dive into low-cost living strategies when it comes to putting a roof over your head. Next, we'll look at investing strategies that will allow you to minimize risk and maximize long-term reward, followed by a discussion of work's purpose in your life. Finally, we'll end with a discussion of a major decision many twentysomethings face: going to grad school.

While there's no formula for success (though do let me know if you find one), I can say that if you follow these principles, you will likely be better off than most in your peer group.

One note about the content of this book: I've geared the

text towards people who have gained basic financial literacy, perhaps by using some of the resources mentioned earlier in this chapter. I don't spend a lot of time on the nitty-gritty of creating a budget, and I don't give many strategies directed at eliminating credit card debt. I'm hoping that readers will at least be familiar with the basics of 401Ks and savings strategies. If you're not, I'd recommend taking a look at *The Total Money Makeover* or *Soldier of Finance* first.

Finally, a quick word on the formatting of this book. First, though the *Chicago Manual of Style* was drilled into me as a history major at the College of William and Mary, I've written this book in a casual, conversational tone. So if you're the type of person who gets irked by sentences ending in a preposition, I'm sorry. Second, my experience in management consulting has taught me the wonderful world of tables, graphs, and charts, so I've made an effort to describe many ideas graphically for all those visual learners out there. Lastly, I've included several breaks in the text in which I describe my own experiences at different points in my early- to mid-twenties. I've included my age and *proportional* net worth at these various points. I've used proportions as opposed to actual dollars and cents to allow the reader to gauge my progress at different points without letting the world know my actual net worth. This is indicated on a scale of $ (lowest net worth) to $$$$$ (highest net worth). These sections look a lot like the one below:

22

Net Worth: $

I grew up in a very fortunate family situation. Though my parents were divorced, they both earned enough to support my brother and me, and we were solidly upper middle class. My parents did not drive Audis or go on lavish vacations to Italy every year. They did, however, own their homes, and my Dad owned a rental property or two (whose lawns I spent many sweaty hours mowing). My brother and I had an old car to drive in high school, and neither of us had to worry about student loans in college. On the other hand, we did not have a trust fund waiting for us, and my parents were not in the position to pull some strings to get us great jobs out of college. Both my brother and I worked at part-time jobs constantly from the time we were 14.

Growing up, I had a polarized view on money. On the one hand, I was very thrifty and saved much of my income, starting with the $20 a week I made as a paper boy. On the other, I haughtily viewed working for money as something that was beneath me. I wanted to be an academic, and I naively thought that I'd never need to earn more than $50,000 per year to support myself. Because of this disdain for money, I actively avoided business classes in college by majoring in history.

It was during my senior year in 2009 that I finally came to terms with my naivety. I was filling out job applications, and to my surprise, people weren't clambering for the chance to interview me for high-paying, fulfilling careers. I looked at my resume, and although it told the story of an accomplished history student, it didn't really speak to meeting the needs of any employers. Though I had a (low) paying job lined up, I stood on the precipice of my college years and looked out into the working life that awaited me. I felt a momentary wave of panic wash over me as I realized how unprepared I really was.

Earlier on, we talked about the future vision you might have for yourself. Whatever that vision may be, this book is intended to give you some of the tools needed to help achieve it. This book is not for people who have no need or desire to be financially independent. It's not for people for whom income doesn't matter due to established family wealth. It's also not for people seeking "get rich quick" schemes or ways to make $9,999 a month from your laptop. This book is aimed at those of us at the start of our careers for whom options abound. This book is for those who are seeking guidance on choosing the right path. This book is also for those of us who want to someday *choose* to work, rather than *need* to work. If you're interested in that last point, read on.

CHAPTER ONE

Save More, Spend Less

"Rather go to bed without dinner than to rise in debt" – Ben Franklin

Three months after signing a lease on a great new apartment my friend and her partner shared together, she lost her job. She's a registered nurse, the demand for which is ever increasing nowadays, so this was an unforeseen event to put it mildly – if anyone was to lose his or her job, they thought it'd be her partner. She was crushed, and I felt for her: losing a job is an emotionally devastating experience. For most Americans, the stress of financial pressures from a job loss compounds upon the emotional distress, forming a brutal one-two punch that many families struggle to fully recover from. Thankfully, this couple could worry less about the financial impact and more about restoring my friend's confidence and career trajectory.

Why were finances not a major concern for them? No, they didn't have a trust fund they could draw upon, and no, one of them hadn't invented an app that had made them independently wealthy. They didn't receive support from their parents, though of course they offered. They weathered this financial storm because they had both been preparing for this potential event: they each had over six months' living expenses available in boring old savings accounts.

Though I was just finishing college at the time of the 2008/2009 financial crisis, I can understand how people became so scared about their futures. A bankrate.com survey of 1,000 adults in 2013 showed that only 23% of those surveyed had sufficient funds to cover six months of expenses. Fifty percent had less than three months' worth, and 27% had *no savings at all.* Back in 2009, at a point in time when half a million jobs were lost *per month*, many people found they had no Plan B but unemployment insurance, which pays a pittance compared to most peoples' monthly expenses.

As I turn to my own generation, which entered the job market during and after the Great Recession, things aren't looking much better. In November 2014 the *Wall Street Journal* found that the savings rate for adults under age 35 was a pitiful negative 2%, meaning that millennials actually spend 2% more than they earn. Now, many of us are still struggling with crippling student loan debt and lackluster job prospects, but still – the numbers are bleak.

How did we get to this point? Blame could be placed on our sense of entitlement, our obsession with consumer products like smartphones, our desire to live in hip, expensive urban neighborhoods, the exploding cost of college, or the crappy job market many of us have experienced throughout the years. The fact is, the cause doesn't matter – what matters is what we can do about it.

This chapter makes the case for saving: it covers the why

and also the how. Saving here does not mean scraping together $1,000 so you can go on that vacation to Puerto Rico, and it does not mean putting just a few percentage points of your monthly income into an account to check a life "to-do" box. Nowhere will you find a guide to organizing a Kickstarter fund. This is serious saving: socking away 20, 30, or 40% of your income, primarily for three reasons: security, opportunity, and freedom.

More on that last point later. First, let's take a look at how far behind you already are.

The Average Net Worth for the Above Average Person

Many people, millennial or not, consider themselves above average. We grew up in environments where getting a C in school might as well have been an F. In fact, a YouGov poll found that the average American considers himself smarter than the average American!

It's no surprise, then, to find this assumption of success and lack of urgency applied to personal finances. Diligently earning paychecks, paying bills, and contributing 4% of one's pay to retirement are often considered "ahead of the curve." No wonder the average 55+ American has just an estimated $150,000 saved, according to a recent report from Personal Capital. Though it might seem substantial, that amount would last maybe five or ten years in retirement.

Let's take a look at what a truly "above average" person's net worth would look like. One of the websites I've found most useful in my quest for achieving financial independence is www.financialsamurai.com, run by fellow William & Mary alumnus Sam Dogen.

To Dogen, an "above average" person is one who:

1) Went to college and got good grades
2) Does not irrationally spend more than he or she makes
3) Saves for the future
4) Takes responsibility for his or her own actions
5) Enjoys empowering himself or herself through learning, whether it be through blogs, magazines, online courses, or other resources
6) Has little-to-no student debt due to scholarships, part-time work, or help from parents (he points out that many in the Baby Boomer generation have benefited from the largest bull market in history, so it's understandable they'd want to help out)

Let's now see what the "above average" person should have saved, by age, for retirement:

THE AVERAGE NET WORTH OF THE ABOVE AVERAGE PERSON

Age	Years Worked	Average Net Worth (Low End)	Average Net Worth (High End)
22	0	$0	$0
23	1	$13,000	$28,000
24	2	$35,500	$58,000
25	3	$58,000	$100,000
30	8	$192,500	$308,000
35	13	$338,000	$520,000
40	18	$475,500	$845,000
45	23	$628,000	$1,200,000
50	28	$765,500	$1,715,000
55	33	$918,000	$2,450,000
60	38	$1,070,500	$3,290,000
65	43	$1,243,000	$4,500,000

Source: FinancialSamurai.com

The above estimates assume the person contributes the maximum ($18,000) in a tax-deferred 401K plan each year after the first year of work. The estimates also assume a 0% return for the low end and a 5% annual return for the high end. Finally, the model assumes a home purchase at age 27 or 28.

Find your age in the table above, then track over to the last two columns to see the average total net worth you should have. Are you above average?

Security, Opportunity, and Freedom: Things Only Savings Can Buy

Generation "Me" is notoriously consumerist: every year we wait for the latest product unveiling from Apple/Microsoft/Victoria's Secret, etc. We live in the moment—in the here and now. We go to happy hours during the week and brunches at the hippest spots during the weekends. We buy tickets to Taylor Swift concerts. We rent apartments in trendy neighborhoods. We prioritize traveling and seeing the world over nearly everything else. All of the above cost money, and that's OK - if we don't use the money we make, it's just pieces of paper in the end, right? However, while these purchases may make us happy in the short-term, what effects might they have on our long-term happiness?

When most people talk about saving, they begrudgingly acknowledge that it might be important someday, but it's not doing a whole lot for them in the here and now. But I would argue that savings *do* buy you something right now. In fact, saving buys you three things very important to our current wellbeing and future success: first, it buys security; second, opportunity; and third, freedom.

Security: The first is pretty obvious. By now, you've

probably heard how important saving up an emergency fund is from many sources, which may include CNN, NPR, and your mom. At least six months' living expenses (which include rent, food, health insurance, etc.) are needed to protect against job loss, major medical expenses, and other unforeseen events. But again, to those of us steeped in honors who always had a spot in games of musical chairs and awards for participation growing up, the thought of failure or adversity is completely alien: a job loss or medical emergency is almost inconceivable. Plus, if something did happen, our Baby Boomer parents would bail us out, right?

Well, the nature of the unexpected is that it defies our perception, and the nature of crisis is that it disrupts our normal operations. Maybe you're excelling in your job at an established company when business slows down and they're forced to lay off thousands, including you. Perhaps you work at a start-up that fails to gain additional funding, leaving you without a source of income. Maybe your parents are not wealthy or even middle class and/or maybe you don't have a good relationship with them, so they're unable to help you out after a job loss. It's very likely that your monthly expenses now exceed what you'd get from unemployment benefits, if you're even eligible. Now what?

This is the moment when six months of savings starts paying for itself. This is also what saving for an emergency fund has bought you up until this point: the comfort of knowing that if things completely go to shit, you won't be immediately out on the street. You can't put a price on that.

Opportunity: This one is a little more abstract. Let's say your college roommate runs into you at a bar one night. You haven't talked for five years, but you strike up a conversation anyways. He tells you he's been working on a new app. You try it out, and it's rough but amazing: potentially the next Twitter or Uber. He says he's just getting off the ground and is still looking for some start-up money. He offers you 1% of his company for $5,000. You look at your bank account balance, which has three digits instead of four, and shrug.

This is an extreme example, of course, but not completely unrealistic. Maybe a more visceral example would be if there's a sudden drop in the stock market that you're pretty sure is temporary – a great time to invest for the ride up. An even more realistic example would be an employer offering you an amazing job in another city that would require you to buy out your current apartment lease.

All of the above are opportunities that cost money. The opportunities range from potentially life-changing to just plain advantageous, but none of them can be achieved without some significant cash saved up.

Obviously, this part of your savings should be separate from your true rainy day fund. I'm not saying you should go out to a bar and invest in the next app developer you find. However, as the old saying goes, you can't make money without spending money, and you can't spend money you haven't saved first.

Freedom: In the land of the free, it's amazing how many people are financially beholden to others through debt. As mentioned earlier, this book assumes you've already taken the steps needed to reduce and eliminate debts – if not, Dave Ramsey and many other authors have excellent resources on how to do so. However, I'll briefly touch on another way saving gives you freedom beyond throwing off the shackles of debt: passive, secure income.

Think about what you have to do right now in your life. You probably *have* to work this week, even if it's at a job you hate, so you can pay bills and meet other financial obligations. You might have student loans or a mortgage which you *have* to pay as falling into default will cripple your financial future. You may *have* to stay in a city you don't particularly like because you're tied to your job. You might also *have* to postpone or cancel vacations or trips you had planned because work gets too busy. Pretty soon, you might find that you're approaching 65 with a lot of hours of your life worked to satisfy obligations. I would argue that a life lived paycheck-to-paycheck is little more than indentured servitude, except for the fact that at least indentured servants had some job security.

What if this didn't *have* to be true, though? What if, eventually, you could save enough money that your passive income streams through interest, dividends, and rental income cover all your basic expenses? You could choose your employer instead of your employer choosing you. You could work on something that has high personal value but little monetary value, or you could choose not to work at all. That is the true definition of financial freedom. What if you didn't have to wait until you're 65 to achieve this life?

Though such an outcome is far from certain and requires years of planning and a good deal of luck, it's not even remotely possible without saving as the first step.

22

Net worth: $$

I'll admit: saving does come naturally to me, largely because of the influence of my parents. I'd often accompany my Dad on trips to garage sales and discount retailers as he tirelessly sought the best deal on something he needed. He is a ruthless negotiator and knows how to get the best price on any purchase, big or small. Though she also appreciates a good discount, my Mom taught me different lessons about financial responsibility: she fastidiously tracks spending and aims to avoid as many major expenses as possible. Due to their influence, as I was growing up I knew I had to spend less than I made: even though I wouldn't call my part-time jobs as a paper boy, drug store clerk, and summer maintenance worker high-paying, I still saved enough so that I rarely if ever had to ask my parents for money to go to the movies or to put gas in my car.

I graduated college in 2009 during a time when the economy was shedding hundreds of thousands of jobs per month. I somehow found a job paying $30,000 per year with benefits, but I still knew I'd need to save up a cushion due to my limited job security.

In the first few years out of college, however, this is really easy to do. Just spend like you're still a broke college student! As I did in college, I did everything I could to acquire the things I needed in the cheapest way possible. I dumpster-dove my first TV, a 15" CRT that somehow still worked. I found furniture for free off craigslist. I brought my lunch to work every day, without fail. I didn't work in a hip part of town, so after-work happy hours were few and far between, limiting the money I spent on entertainment. When I did go out, it was often to a friend's house party that usually just cost me the price of a six pack of beer. I also got creative when going on dates, often opting to walk in the park or go to farmer's markets instead of buying expensive dinners. I didn't do any automatic payroll deductions or other often-suggested strategies to save: I just lived as if I was still on a college student's budget.

Despite my meager income, this mindset helped me save a

six-month emergency fund in a little over a year.

Nice to Have versus Need to Have

Most personal finance resources will instruct you to set up a savings strategy. These usually range from the pretty mild ("set up an automatic 5% deduction to go towards your savings from your paycheck") to the extreme ("live on less than $20,000 per year, including housing costs, no matter what"). The saying is always "pay yourself first," with little explanation about what that actually means.

These approaches are not one-size-fits-all. The investment banker doesn't *need* to live on $20K per year, just like someone making $35K shouldn't *just* be saving 5% of his income if he wants to be financially secure someday. People need to tailor their savings strategies to their individual goals, personal identities, and specific living situations, which is why I emphasize everyone should determine their "why" before embarking on any lifestyle change.

However, there is one approach to saving that everyone can adopt, no matter the circumstance. That approach involves dividing your desires into "nice-to-haves" and "need-to-haves." The first step for anyone getting serious about saving is deciding which expenses fall within each bucket.

Need-to-haves are pretty straightforward. These are the basics needed to function that are most important to you. Food, housing, student loan payments, transportation costs, and clothing all fall into this category. Again, the actual amounts could vary tremendously depending on an individual's budget, but these are the things that are not optional.

Nice-to-haves are often known by another name:

discretionary spending. These items not only include someone's "fun budget" but also optional things that replace items you can get for free. For instance: maybe you prefer $5 Starbucks lattes to the free coffee available at your office, or perhaps you like buying first class upgrades on flights. Maybe you decide to take an Uber to the airport instead of cashing in an IOU with a friend who has a car. Whatever it is, it's either nonessential or a more expensive alternative for something essential.

The savings strategy outlined in this book relies on limiting both of these categories but in different ways. For need-to-have purchases, strive to find less costly replacements that provide similar value. For nice-to-have purchases, reduce or eliminate those that do not provide sufficient value to justify their costs.

As mentioned above, there are categories of expenses that one must have: food, shelter, transportation, etc. However, within each of these categories, there's significant flexibility in how that need is met. This strategy gets to the principle of *substitute goods*, which states that all else being equal, consumers will prefer lower cost options when deciding between similar goods. The closer the price, the more similar the two items need to be: few people would choose biking over driving if they were roughly the same cost; however, if the price of fuel increases to the extent that driving is much, much more expensive than biking, more people may switch from driving to biking. The same principle can be applied to your personal finances.

List out all your critical expenses and what you pay for them. Next to each, think of a less costly alternative that meets that same need, then calculate the annual savings. Let's take a look at how the need-to-have strategy might shake out for a typical early 20s recent college graduate:

Essential Item	Estimated Yearly Cost	Less Costly Alternative	Estimated Alternative Yearly Cost	Savings Potential
Rent for one-bedroom apartment	$18,000	Rent in shared group house	$9,600	$8,400
Car (including gas)	$4,100	Public transit	$1,200	$2,900
Lunch at work	$2,500	Bring bag lunch	$650	$1,850
Gym membership	$1,200	Free weights	$100	$1,100
Ikea furniture	$600	Craigslist/Hand-me-down	$200	$400
			Total:	$14,650

So the first step of building your savings machine is starting with the fundamentals: optimize your need-to-have expenses, since these are often the highest.

Now that we've seen how to squeeze savings out of need-to-haves, let's turn to nice-to-haves. If recent data hold any truth, this is the area the millennial generation struggles the most.

Gallup's August 2014 survey of Americans in different age groups revealed some telling signs of this trend. In the survey, higher percentages of Millennials reported spending more on leisure activities and clothing than other age groups. A majority of this group also reported spending more in 2014 than the year prior, again a higher percentage than other ages. Further, more millennials were increasing their spending on rent than other age groups. In 2012, when unemployment was among its highest for new grads, Millennials spent an average of $784 on discretionary spending per month and started riots outside retail malls to get pairs of $200 limited-edition Air Jordan sneakers.

Some will say that millennials have fewer financial responsibilities like kids, mortgages, and ailing parents, allowing them to spend more of their income on discretionary items. To me, however, this is just squandered opportunity.

This book relies on the principal of delayed gratification, which, granted, is a pretty deflating term. I think a better way to describe this is "give up a little now for a lot more later on." For many, it's hard to abandon short-term thinking in favor of a long-term plan. It's not easy to suggest staying in instead of going on a bar crawl. It's also not too fun to pack a lunch every morning instead of going to that sandwich shop you like down the street from your work. However, discretionary spending to satisfy short-term wants can have a seriously detrimental effect on long-term desires.

To visualize this effect, let's go back to the $14,650 in savings we identified earlier. This is certainly a hefty sum from any perspective. However, take a look at how much this amount would grow over 10 years if you were able to invest it in something that returned just 3% per year:

Principal	Annual Return	Term (years)	Ending Amount
$14,650	3%	10	$ 19,688

Not too bad. Now, let's say you invested this money in the stock market, for which the average annual return is about 7%:

Principal	Annual Return	Term (years)	Ending Amount
$14,650	3%	10	$ 19,688
$14,650	7%	10	$ 28,819

You just doubled your money! I know 10 years seems an indeterminable amount of time to most readers, but as someone who is approaching his 10-year high school reunion, I can tell you it goes more quickly than you'd think.

Keep in mind that the above analysis just looks at a *single year* of cost savings: in other words, after living a life of austerity for a year, this person reverted completely to his old ways and still realized a pretty good return on his savings. However, what if he instead saved an average of $10,000 *per year* over those 10 years, obtaining an average return of 3%? Here's what that accumulated savings would look like:

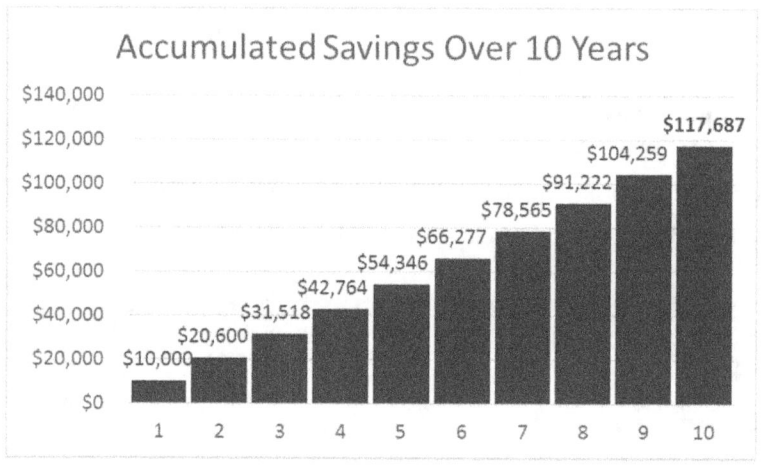

This is the benefit of not living paycheck-to-paycheck, and this is what financial gurus mean when they recommend "pay yourself first." *On average, each dollar not spent during this 10 year period is worth about $1.17 at the end of the period.* That may not seem like a lot at the moment, but this snowball effect really adds up over time.

Let's turn back to discretionary spending. We've been using the example of finding cheaper replacements for the essentials, and I hope you've seen the substantial impact this can have on your long-term security. However, there's even more opportunity for savings when looking at non-essential spending.

After you've completed the above table for essential spending, make another one for your discretionary items. List some of the major categories of your discretionary spend, which might include brunches, bar tabs, and vacations in the first column along with their costs in the second column. Think up less-costly alternatives with associated costs in the next two columns as before. Here's where it will differ: in the next column, assign a "happiness score" of one to five for each category based on how important this item is. Think long and hard about how much actual joy you derive from this purchase: is it something that brings regular fulfillment to your life, or does it provide more fleeting happiness (retail therapy)? Lastly, create a new column labeled "minimum spend possible." This is the minimum amount you're willing to pay for this category. It may be $0 for some categories and more for others.

This might look something like the below for a twentysomething:

Discretionary Item	Estimated Annual Cost	Less Costly Alternative	Alternative Cost	Happiness Score (5=most, 1=least)	Savings (Alternative Option)
International travel	$3,000	Domestic travel	$800	5	$2,200
Bar tabs	$1,200	House parties	$200	3	$1,000
Brunches and restaurants	$3,000	Eating in	$1,500	3	$1,500
Daily Starbucks latte	$1,250	Drip coffee at home	$120	2	$1,130
New iPad	$600	Use old laptop	$0	2	$600
Designer shoes	$200	Discount shoes	$50	1	$150
Cable TV	$1,200	Internet TV	$600	1	$600
				Total:	$7,180

Clearly, someone can't completely give up something like going to happy hours in favor of always having apartment parties, and it's pretty likely you'll eat out at least a few times over the course of the year. For these categories, the tool demonstrates the difference in the two extremes. However, other categories, like cable TV, *can* be completely cut out. Further, this tool assigns a qualitative rank to each item, ensuring that costs are optimally in line with satisfaction. Start with the bottom of the list when looking for expenses to cut.

Implementing lower-cost living isn't easy, especially if you're used to spending as you please. Once you've identified savings opportunities, it's really easy to slip back into previous habits. That's why adopting a lower cost lifestyle requires a change in *mindset*. Just as my Dad would shop around at multiple stores, before making a purchase, ask yourself: "is this the least expensive way to satisfy this want or need?" Celebrate "zero dollar days" when you go through a whole 24 hours without spending a dime. Finally, as mentioned before, make sure you have a long-term goal that gives a reason for your thriftiness to keep you on track.

23

Net worth: $$

We've talked a lot about replacement goods: replacing something that meets a need for something else that meets the same need at a lower cost, a strategy valid for both need-to-have and nice-to-have purchases. I know of few better examples of this principle than car costs.

As I've mentioned previously, I was very fortunate in that my family is well off and solidly upper-middle class. I don't have a trust fund, but I never had to worry about food and shelter, and my parents generously paid my college tuition while I paid for books and meals. One of the most generous things my parents have done for me is to buy me a car when I graduated from college. I spent the summer of 2009 researching different makes and models, test driving cars, and trying to decide whether I liked the color Gunmetal Blue better than Meteor Grey. I finally settled on a sporty Mazda 3, which was everything I could've wanted in a car – I loved every moment of driving when I had it from 2009 to 2011.

When I was 23, I got a higher-paying job in downtown Washington, DC and moved into a very affordable room in a five-bedroom house in the suburbs. There was one problem: it was next to impossible to drive to my job due to horrendous traffic, so I had to explore public transit options.

After I moved into the shared group house and found I'd be commuting into the city, the Mazda went from a luxurious utility good to just a nice-to-have luxury. I realized that at most I'd be using the car once or twice a week while paying nearly $150 per month in insurance and gas. I also needed to add in the cost of maintenance, car registration and inspection, and all the other little costs that accrue over time. I then thought about how I could invest the value of the car in something that at least maintained its value (as opposed to depreciated in value) over time. So I decided to sell my graduation present.

Not having a car is a very hard adjustment at first – things like trips to the grocery store or Target are suddenly huge ordeals, especially if you live in a less-than-walkable suburb like I did at the time. Hardship often breeds creativity and innovation, however, and I became an expert in alternative modes of travel. I leveraged the county's excellent bus system for the first time, which would take me to grocery stores, barber shops, and the subway station. I also outfitted my bike so that it could carry groceries and other items, allowing me to simultaneously do errands and get exercise when the weather was nice. I took advantage of my company's tax-advantaged transit program to lower my subway fare costs. When I did need to drive, I used car share programs like Zipcar. A year in, I had nearly forgotten about the cool-blue Mazda hatchback that I used to jet around the city in.

At the time of this writing, I've fortunately advanced in my career and grown my income, but I still do not own a car. Though it's far easier to do now that I live in a walkable area, I rely on public transit, and I bike to work every day the weather allows. I secretly do want to buy another Mazda 3 once having a car is a need-to-have again as opposed to a nice-to-have, but for now, I don't need it.

I've always attributed selling my car as one of the major reasons for my relative financial success in my 20s (the other you can read about in the "Never Live Alone" chapter), but I've never actually done the math on it until now. Taking the simple substitute good table from above, here's what the financial impact has looked like over the past four years:

Discretionary item	Estimated Annual Costs	Less Costly Alternative	Alternative Cost
Car		Bike/Bus	
Gas	$750	Bike	$50
Insurance	$1,300	Bus fare	$300
Maintenance	$500	Subway fare	$900
Depreciation (of the car's value)	$1,200		
Annual Car Cost Total:	**$3,750**	**Annual Alternative Total:**	**$1,250**
		Total Annual Savings:	**$2,500**
		Years:	4
		Total Cost Difference Over 4 Years:	$10,000
		Interest from Sale Proceeds Over 4 Years:	$1,100
		Total Financial Benefit:	**$11,100**

The savings can be even greater if you have a car loan and associated monthly payment and if you're able to bike to and from work instead of taking public transit at all. If I had a $250 monthly car payment and found a way to bike to work every day instead of taking the metro, my cost savings over four years would have been an estimated $23,000. Though everyone's circumstances are different, a report from American Public Transportation Association estimates that savings for the average driver who gives up driving for alternate modes of travel could be as much as $10,000 per year, which certainly pays a lot of bills.

Why Some "Well-Off" People Are Actually Poor

One of the great mysteries to modern life is the fact that some middle class, upper middle class, and even wealthy families still live paycheck-to-paycheck. Undoubtedly, the higher cost of housing and education relative to incomes has contributed to this: a lawyer making $100,000 per year may not feel rich if he is still servicing a $1,700 per month student loan debt. However, I think the problem is more related to consumerism. Specifically, the issue stems from people viewing income as an expense ceiling as opposed to a vehicle for long-term happiness. Broadly, people's attitude towards spending seems to coalesce across three major ways of thinking.

The most dangerous form of thinking is "I could afford x good if I only did y," which drives debt spending and represents the ultimate in short-term thinking. An example might be someone making the minimum payment on his or her credit card and still purchasing new clothes from Banana Republic, all the while racking up debt and interest.

A more reasonable mindset many people have instead is "I make x amount, so I can afford y." A good example is a new grad who figures she can afford a $1,400 per month studio apartment on a $3,500 per month salary. This approach won't necessarily bankrupt someone, but it is not the way to build wealth. The mindset is especially problematic when a person's income increases, which is often a signal to increase consumption based on affordability. Even though more and more goods are obtained, net worth may stay relatively constant.

The third mindset completely separates income from expenses by asking "My income is x, and my expenses are y, so how can I maximize x and minimize y?" This is the approach that generates cash flow which is a prerequisite to building wealth and financial security.

Let's look at how each of these approaches might affect a

person's net worth over time:

Net Worth Over 5 Years Under Different Spending Mindsets

Mindset A: "I could afford x if I only did y"

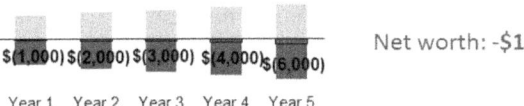

Net worth: -$16,000

Mindset B: "I make x, so I can afford y"

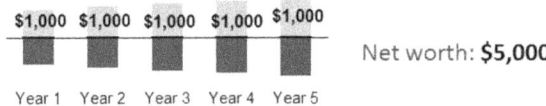

Net worth: **$5,000**

Mindset C: "How can I maximize income x and minimize expenses y?"

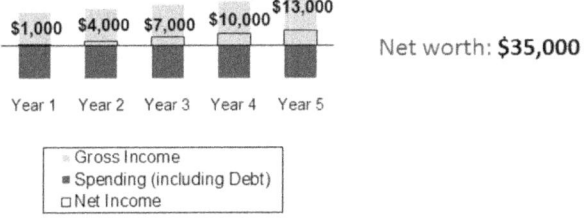

Net worth: **$35,000**

The incomes in all of the examples above are the same: the only thing that changes is the amount spent each year. In the first example, expenses increase at a faster rate than income, generating more and more debt (a "debt pileup"). In the second example, expenses rise in lockstep with income, resulting in a meager savings each year that at least results in a positive net worth. In the third example, expenses stay constant as income rises, resulting in a robust $35,000 net worth figure.

The amounts above are purely hypothetical, but I hope

they illustrate the importance of having the right mindset when it comes to income and expenses. Even if you earn a good salary, you're really not wealthy (or even financially secure) if you are allowing your expenses to increase parallel to your pay.

A second reason why many high-earners are not necessarily wealthy is related to the relationship between assets and liabilities. I know of no one who explains this better than Robert Kiyosaki, author of *Rich Dad, Poor Dad*. In his book, Kiyosaki explains that liabilities are any purchases that do not produce income or a return on investment, while assets are purchases that do.

It's easy to view spending money on restaurant dinners, cars, a house, health insurance, and index funds as all the same thing: these items all take cash out of your pocket. However, some of these offer the opportunity to return that cash (sometimes, even with interest), and the others don't.

Restaurant dinners offer no return other than your happy belly. A car will maintain some value over time but depreciates quickly and generates other expenses related to maintenance, fuel, and insurance. Clothing also offers no monetary return. These are all liabilities – they may meet needs, but they do not put cash back into your pocket.

By contrast, let's consider an index fund purchase. While it's definitely possible it could lose value, that purchase will generate dividend income and offer the potential for price appreciation, something a car purchase certainly won't do. While Kyosaki maintains that a house is more a liability than an asset, this item will typically hold its value – it also reduces housing costs compared to rent, which is a form of return on investment. A purer example is rental property, which not only maintains its value (meaning you can typically sell it for at least the amount you paid) but also generates income in the form of rent. This and the rest of the above are assets.

In most people's imaginations, rich means driving around Porsches and spending thousands of dollars on clothes and vacations. That indeed may be the image of wealth for CEOs and entrepreneurs. However, as books like *The Middle Class Millionaire* and *The Millionaire Next Door* tell us, wealth doesn't need to look like this. There are people who are rich who drive used Honda civics, live in modest houses in the suburbs, and don't own a single yacht. These people are rich because they've minimized their liabilities and maximized their assets. They're rich because they are *financially independent*, meaning that they *choose* to work and don't *need* to work. I'm not sure we could say the same for an indebted CEO who spends all of his or her money on cars, yachts, vacation homes, and the like: even that high-income individual is potentially only a job loss away from poverty.

The balance between saving and spending comes down to what a person values. If keeping up with the Joneses through ever increasing purchases of cars, boats, clothes, and other liabilities is what's important, then that's what a person will spend money on. If "living in the moment" is a person's life philosophy, then that life may be filled with high spending on material goods and credit card debt. Though this person might feel alive with every incremental purchase, is that really the best path to enduring happiness?

Or, alternatively, a person could value security, opportunity, and freedom. A person with this mindset will have an objective: obtain financial freedom at some point in my life so that I can do what's most important to me. That dream could be a homestead in rural New England, like the authors of the Frugal Woods blog. That dream could be having time to spend with a son or daughter as he or she grows up. Whatever that dream may be, these individuals understand that achieving it requires some sacrifices now for a big return later on.

CHAPTER TWO

Never Live Alone

Sharing is caring…about your financial future

Most of us remember those first few moments of college when you arrived at your dorm room, your new home, for the first time. Either you got there first and anxiously awaited your roommate's arrival, or you barged in, parents in tow, just as your roomie was unpacking. As we glanced about the 200 square foot room, we thought, "How the hell am I going to share this space with another person?"

Fast forward four years, and while it may not have become natural to share a single bedroom with one (or two) other people (especially if one of them was a little crazy), most of us had adapted to a new definition of personal space. Even those lucky enough to have had a private bedroom still usually shared a kitchen, common area, and laundry room.

Ever given thought as to why colleges cram students into small spaces like sardines? No, it's not because they think it builds "character." The answer is that it's very *cost efficient* for the college to do so through the simple principle of economies of scale. Since running a dormitory is mostly sunk costs, doubling and tripling up students allows administrators to maximize dormitory capacity, meaning they achieve a higher return on their "investment" in dormitories with more tuition-paying students for the same fixed costs. In a dorm with double-occupancy rooms, each student pays a lower share of his housing cost than he would if a dorm was filled with singles.

So, since this seems to be a good way for a college to optimize student fees, why can't we apply the same methodology to our own post-college living situations?

22

Net worth: $

After graduating college the previous May and completing a summer program, I moved to Washington, DC in September of 2009. Despite the country being in the worst depths of the recession, I had somehow scored a job paying the rich sum of $30,000 per year. In the DC area, that meant I needed to develop a pretty tight budget. Luckily, a college friend was living in the area, so I was able to rent the smallest room of a three-bedroom apartment in suburban Maryland for $640 per month. My room even came with a view – of the dumpster.

Living within Your Means vs. Living Below Them

Now, let me back up: I'm not suggesting you go out and try to get into the Guinness Book of World Records for most unrelated individuals living in a single room. However, the title of this chapter, "Never Live Alone," gets at a core theme of this book: not only should you live within your means, you should live as far *below* them as possible. A great way to achieve that goal is to live with roommates.

When you graduate college, you basically have three options for housing. First, you can move back in with your parents -- this may be your only option if you majored in something like 14ᵗʰ Century Medieval Architecture. Though some families may be less open to this than others, this is a viable option for the majority of college kids. Furthermore, much of the stigma associated with this option has diminished due to the financial crisis of 2008-2011, though you're still probably not going to go bragging to your friends about your sweet digs in mom's basement.

The second option, if you're lucky enough to land a job, is setting out on your own and renting a studio or one-bedroom apartment. This is a great option if walking around in your underwear while cooking is a priority for you. Studios give you privacy and living arrangements that you can truly call "your place."

Finally, your third option is to shack up with a roommate (or three). Not an option most would consider ideal, but hey, at least you're not living with Mom and Dad, right?

Now, most people would make this decision based on what they can afford. So, say one recent college grad, Beth, snags a job as a sales associate in Chicago paying $3,000 per month. She might look for a two bedroom to share with her best friend for $1,000 in rent. Beth's friend, Dave, works as a financial analyst pulling in $4,000 per month. He knows he's not supposed to spend more than 1/3 of his income on housing, so he's looking at studios and one-bedrooms in a popular part of town in the $1,200-$1,500 range.

However, this decision should not be made on *affordability* but rather *efficiency*. Efficiency in this context maximizes benefit and minimizes cost. Using this mindset, Beth might instead choose to live in a group house with three others for $500 per month or even live at home. Dave might decide to split a three bedroom with three other guys, costing him $700 per month. With these options, Beth and Dave are effectively paying themselves in exchange for giving up some personal space.

We've all heard the rule of thumb that you shouldn't spend more than a third of your income on housing. Technically speaking, both Dave and Beth started out adhering to this rule of thumb. But how much could either of them really save to get ahead under that basic guideline? After factoring in groceries, student loans, car payments, and gas: not much.

Any personal finance resource worth its salt will recommend you build an emergency fund worth 3-6 months of expenses. If you are like I was as a new college grad, your emergency fund is approximately $100. In Beth's situation, she could save $5,000 for her emergency fund in just 5 months if she lived at home instead of splitting a two-bedroom. Dave could save this amount in 10 months by choosing his less costly option.

However, since their rents are lower with the low cost options, their expenses (and therefore their emergency fund goals) are lower as well. Even if Beth saved the same amount of money ($500) each month in both the two-bedroom and group house options, her emergency fund goal for the group house is only $1,500-$3,000, while for her two-bedroom option she'd need $3,000-$6,000 to cover her higher rent for 3-6 months. She'll reach her emergency fund goal with the group house much sooner, lowering her risk if an unforeseen event like a job loss happens. Moreover, spending less on rent allows Beth to invest more in assets that can start generating a return for her.

24

Net worth: $$

After two years of living in a 3BR, my roommates were going their separate ways to move in with their significant others (more on that later). I had changed jobs a few months prior, so I had a little more purchasing power with my $45,000 salary. I started looking for an apartment closer to my work in downtown Washington, DC.

I knew it was going to be tough when the first open house I attended attracted a crowd of thirty people milling outside the apartment, anxiously awaiting the viewing. When the landlord came to announce someone had put a deposit on the unit already without even seeing it, many people nevertheless still took the tour. I overheard some apartment hunters trying to negotiate with the landlord to pay a higher rent for the privilege of living there.

Knowing that I wanted to keep my expenses as low as possible, I took a look at some group houses in some of the trendier neighborhoods of DC like Mount Pleasant and Columbia Heights. Demand was so high that the existing tenants held formal interviews with dozens of applicants. One $1,000 room I looked at was in a house with a single bathroom shared by six people. Another $800 room was a basement closet that had easy access to the sump pump right by the foot of the bed.

So, I retooled my expectations. I started looking at group houses further out in the suburbs. Finally, I found one that seemed like a great deal: a bedroom in a five-bedroom house in suburban Maryland right by NIH. Since it was in a not-so-convenient location, I was actually able to lower my rent from my previous $640 to $450 after I signed the lease.

Many people, when they get a new job or promotion at work, look at what else they can buy with their new income. Maybe it's a nicer car, more convenient apartment, or that handbag they've had their eye on. However, if you want to get ahead, you need to take the opposite tack: what expenses can you reduce to maximize your monthly margin?

As you saw from the previous chapter, rent is the single most expensive item in a typical person's budget. A common cliché I hear among my peers is that "my first paycheck goes to my landlord, then my second is the one I use for everything else." Many millennials in New York City, Boston, and San Francisco pay 40, 50, or 60% of their gross earnings to rent. I've had friends who have been forced to move every year because their landlords boosted their rent 10-15% after their lease expired. At best, this is a road to living paycheck-to-paycheck; at worst, this could lead to substantial debt.

It's clear many in our millennial generation want to live in hip neighborhoods with lots of bars, restaurants, and basic staples like grocery stores within walking distance. Those neighborhoods are great – I happen to live in one now, and I love it. But if you want to live anything other than paycheck-to-paycheck, you should be looking at the most affordable living situation as opposed to the most accommodating, especially when you're first starting out.

Personal Benefits of Roommates: Strive for the DINK Lifestyle

We've discussed the financial benefits of living with roommates. Now let's look at the personal benefits of roommate living.

Some of you might be saying, "personal *benefits?* Like your roommates leaving dirty dishes out or coming home drunk at 2am?" Yes, oddly enough, I am talking about those, because people who share their personal space learn to do something that's critical to their future success: compromise.

26

Net worth: $$$$$

By mid-2012, I had spent a year in the group house. Due to low rent, sharing utility bills, selling my car in favor of taking public transit, and increasing my salary moderately, I was well on my way to my savings goal.

The first year was trying. While there were five bedrooms in the house, six people actually lived there, since a couple lived in the master bedroom. That meant that six people often wanted to use the kitchen, watch TV, and do laundry, and the times we wanted to do those things often coincided. Moreover, I shared my bathroom with another roommate.

How did we all get along? We compromised and communicated. My bath-mate and I took turns cleaning the shower and sink. If someone was cooking, we'd let that person finish before someone else started dinner. The housemates divvied up tasks like vacuuming the brown 1960s shag carpet and collecting six different checks for each of four different utility bills. If someone wanted to watch a show on the living room TV and someone else was currently using that TV, those two people compromised. If something bothered one of us, we made sure to communicate our concerns. Because we compromised in our living situation, we all were able to share in the savings of living in that affordable rental house.

Eventually, some roommates moved out, and new ones moved in. My last year in the house my roommates and I all became pretty good friends. We affectionately nicknamed the house the "Chateau du Bro," watched movies together, and even had whiskey tastings from time to time.

After 3 ½ years in the house, it was finally time to move out and live with my significant other. A lot of couples struggle with sharing personal space when they live together for the first time. However, since my partner and I had both learned to compromise and communicate in our living situations (she also lived in a group house), living together is a breeze.

Living with other people teaches you a lot about compromise. Also, for those moving to a city in which they don't know anyone, it can be an easy source of friends. However, from my view, one of the best personal benefits of living with random people not related to you is that you become well-prepared to live with a significant other.

In her book *The Defining Decade: Why Your Twenties Matter and How to Make the Most of Them Now*, Dr. Meg Jay asserts that although those of us in our twenties think we have a lot of time to kill, we really don't. More than half of Americans are married or are dating or living with their future partners by age 30. For many of us, a personal and emotional objective throughout our twenties is to find someone with whom to settle down. My assertion is that doing so not only benefits your emotional well-being, but also your financial one, through the simple DINK concept: Double Income No Kids.

This should be the payoff for living with multiple roommates for years, because as much money as you can potentially save through economies of scale in a group house, this pales in comparison to the savings two income earners achieve by sharing a single apartment.

Let's go back to our example of Beth and Dave. It turns out Dave is at a bar one night with one of his roommates who introduces him to his lovely friend, Beth. The two hit it off immediately. After a few years of dating, they decide to take the plunge and move in together. Because they delayed gratification and chose lower-cost living options in previous years, they both had significant emergency funds, retirement savings, and other investments. They both looked at their budgets and the housing stock available. Dave still had that $1,500 one-bedroom he was interested in a few years ago in the back of his mind, but when the two started looking, they found an even nicer unit for $1,600 per month with a fireplace, hardwood floors, and a balcony. They sign the lease, and since they split the rent equally, Dave's rent only goes up $100 to $800, and Beth's is bumped up $300 from her previous group house rent. Though they're paying slightly more, they're getting a lot more in return: privacy, amenities, and location. They're both still able to save a good portion of their incomes each month since they haven't yet breached the 1/3 income rule for housing. They continue to get along pretty well, leading to the inevitable popping of the question, and they get married a year later. Since they've been socking so much money away, they find they can afford to put 20% down on a townhouse, which actually substantially decreases their housing expense, since they really only lose the interest, taxes, and homeowners' association dues from their monthly payment (the rest goes to pay back the principal).

Sounds pretty good to be Beth and Dave, right? Well, while their relationship in this book took place over the course of a single paragraph, in real life such an ending requires careful strategic planning and future vision. A prerequisite is accepting delayed gratification by focusing on affordability and cost efficiency as opposed to amenity and convenience when choosing housing options early in one's career. While it certainly involves a bit of luck, looking at apartments as a cost to be minimized as opposed to a good to be enjoyed can supercharge your savings and put you on a better path for the long run.

CHAPTER THREE

You're Not Smarter than Mr. Market

And bad mistakes…I've made a few…

So you've wrangled your expenses and started to maximize your income, allowing you to set increasing amounts of money aside each month for your savings. As your savings start piling up, it's natural to ask the exciting question: "OK, now what do I do with all this cold hard CASH?"

Some people's answer might be to stuff the money away under their mattresses. For others, it might be reason to take their foot off the savings gas pedal and enjoy life (trip to Europe, anyone?). Others still might read a few articles from *Seeking Alpha* or *The Motley Fool* and invest in biotech stocks to try and turn their thousands into tens of thousands. In this last example, I'd just recommend going to your local casino. At least they'll give you free drinks as you gamble your money away.

The answer in this book, at least at first, is a little boring: not a whole lot. This chapter won't cover ways to get rich day-trading stocks or investing in rental properties. We won't be discussing how to start a business from scratch or build an app using your savings. What this chapter will do is set out a multi-tiered strategy for investing that minimizes risk and maximizes long-term return. But before we do that, let's dive into a brief discussion of the relationship between risk and return, as this principle is crucial to implementing a viable investing strategy.

Risk versus Return

Every investment, including savings accounts, involves risk, which is simply defined as "the chance I will receive less than I invested." Every investment should also have an expected return; if it doesn't, it's not an investment! The more perceived risk an investment has, the greater return investors will demand of that asset, and vise-versa. This concept is known as the risk premium.

For instance, prior to the FDIC insuring savings accounts, if a bank went bust, depositors could lose their entire savings, which is why people rioted outside banks during the Great Depression. The chance of that happening today is nil, meaning that investors are willing to accept pitiful interest rates in return for the knowledge that their money is safe. However, savings accounts are subject to a different kind of risk: inflation. If a savings account's interest rate is less than the inflation rate, then the depositor is actually LOSING money in real terms, since those savings can buy fewer and fewer goods over time. In practice, this is not a huge deal, since savings accounts are highly liquid, meaning depositors can easily withdraw their money and invest elsewhere if inflation picks up.

This can be a big deal in another asset: bonds. A bond is a loan in which the investor (you) loans money to another entity (government or corporation), and that entity pays a set percentage of your investment to you each year in compensation. Unlike savings accounts, bond buyers are not allowed to prematurely withdraw their money without a huge penalty. Inflation has a critical effect on bonds: if you buy a bond when inflation (and the interest rate) is low and then inflation starts picking up, you're basically locked into a contract in which you lose money. Conversely, if you buy a bond when inflation and interest rates are high, you could realize substantial profits if those two metrics fall in the future. Sometimes I get really jealous thinking about all those Baby Boomers who bought 30-year bonds in the '80s with interest rates of 20%...

Now, at least with savings accounts and bonds, your initial investment (principal) is guaranteed. That's not the case with stocks. When you buy a share of stock, you're quite literally buying a stake (albeit a tiny one) in a company. The value of a share in a given company is purportedly based on that company's current and future profitability, though in the days of internet companies prices are often set more on expectations than on reality. Today, you could buy 10 shares of Google stock at the current price of $1,000 per share. Tomorrow, Google could announce that they've "won the internet," boosting the price of each share to $1,500, giving you a 50% gain on your investment. On the other hand, Google could say that they've been hacked and all the personal information it's collected about everyone has been released to Russian hackers, causing the stock price to plummet 50%, meaning you've just lost 50% of your investment.

As you can see above, investing in any one stock is pretty risky, even if that stock is Google, which leads to the importance of *diversification*, which spreads an investment (and therefore the risk) across many stocks. This is the idea behind mutual funds and index funds, which invest in tens or hundreds of various companies. Even with these, there is a chance you may lose your investment, so investors often expect a higher annual return of 7-8% to compensate for the higher risk as opposed to the 2-4% typically expected from relatively safe government bonds.

As you can see, considering risk versus return is crucial when making any investment decision.

24

Net worth: $$$

I did not major in finance and had no idea what a stock was until I graduated college. When I was 22, I had saved enough that I could invest $5,000 in an S&P index fund. However, after I super-charged my savings schedule, I found I had more money sitting around than I thought I should, so I looked for ways to put it to work for me.

I started becoming interested in stocks, particularly Apple stock. I read all the stock analysts' reports about Apple and tracked its price on Yahoo! finance. I cashed out my S&P fund (which was up 10%) and decided to put that along with some more of my savings towards individual stocks. Apple was initially a good winner for me – it started rising, though I was so paranoid I would lose money that I jumped in and out of the investment, racking up trading fees in the process. However, I still made money, and I thought to myself "this is easy!"

I found an online trading platform that made trading stocks even easier. Vanguard charged a significant fee for every trade and limited the amount of trades I could make, but this platform would charge only $5, and I could see stock prices move in real time. So I converted my trading account to this new platform. They even gave me an Amazon Kindle Fire for doing so.

At one point, I had invested over half of my total net worth in Apple stock. Even my "Go-Go" mindset of the time could recognize that this was extremely risky, so I sold most of my stake. This was lucky, too, (and I do mean lucky), as Apple started an epic price skid shortly thereafter. I searched for a new investment vehicle, and I found an option that promised even greater returns: biotech stocks. Companies that were developing drugs often realized huge gains if (and that's a big IF) their clinical studies met endpoints that would encourage FDA approval. Since I worked as a health care consultant, I thought I was smarter than everyone else trading these stocks, so I dove in.

These stocks are notoriously volatile, and I rode them up and down in the worst ways. I found I started spending a lot of time reading about and trading stocks, even using my trading platform while I was at work during the day. Every click of the "buy" button released dopamine, and it excited me to the point that I didn't really care that I was losing a lot of money through trading fees and investment losses. I discovered stock options (if you don't know what these are, don't worry, because you should never invest in them) as a way to hedge my investments and multiply my theoretical returns. With every loss, I thought to myself, "next time, I'll have a bigger return, and I can make back my loss and get a profit, too." The classic gambling mindset.

Well, you can guess how this turned out. After about a year and a half of this, I found I had dug myself a deep hole to the tune of several thousands of dollars, to the point that

I'm still deducting those stock losses from my taxes today. Furthermore, I wasn't even trading in tax advantaged accounts, meaning that any profits I would have made would have been taxed anyways.

Obviously, I look back on this period and shudder at all the time and money I wasted chasing the white rabbit. However, I think one irony really crystalizes this for me. Remember that initial $5,000 investment I made in a low-cost S&P index fund? Its current value at the time of this writing would have been approximately $11,000, a return of <u>120%.</u>

Trading versus Investing

The core of my problem, which is also a problem for many people, is that I thought I was smarter than the market – I thought my unique analytical skillset and knowledge would allow me to succeed where others had failed. I went to a good school and got a fair amount of A's, so I must be able to conquer the stock market with some studying, right? This is a very, very dangerous idea for the average investor for the simple reason that trading stocks is a zero-sum game: there is always a winner and always a loser.

Think about what happens when you tell your online brokerage to buy a share of XYZ stock: that broker (which is likely a robot, by the way) will go out into the market to try and find someone selling a share of that stock. That stock (or option) will be priced according to the supply of shares available and demand of people wanting to buy the stock.

Seems simple enough, right? Not quite. While the average retail investor might buy or sell a stock because he is part of a monthly contribution plan or because he read an article or two on *Seeking Alpha*, more often than not the person on the other end of that trade is a *professional trader* whose job is literally to learn everything there is to know about that one stock. All the news, all the quarterly returns, all the macroeconomic factors affecting that stock are all known to this one guy sitting at a Bloomberg terminal. Odds are also that this person is an expert at technical analysis, meaning he can read stock price charts to determine the best times to buy and sell. The average retail investor will be emotionally driven to buy after a long run up in a stock's price ("I need to hitch a ride to this gravy train!") and sell after bad news tanks the stock ("I need to get off this sinking ship!"), but the professional trader will know to sell at the highs and buy at the lows. Today, it's even more likely you're going up against a trading algorithm or robot as opposed to a real person: basically Wall Street terminators whose sole purpose is to make money.

There's one other crucial cost to consider when trading stocks: time. At the peak of my day trading addiction, I would spend hours each day reading stock news, studying technical analysis methods, and researching quarterly reports. That time could have instead been spent studying content directly related to my job, looking for side business ideas, or even just enjoying time with friends and family. If you place a dollar value on your time, say $20 per hour, the costs of researching the stock market add up quickly, especially if you find you're not good at day trading.

Now I'm not saying that people should never purchase individual stocks – buy-and-hold is a viable long-term strategy and will be discussed later in this chapter. However, the next time you get the urge to buy an option or trade in and out of a stock, think of that algorithm-driven Wall Street Terminator staring back at you through your computer monitor from the other side of that trade.

Why the Mattress Strategy Doesn't Work

Now that we've talked a little about risk versus return as well as the absence of a get-rich-quick scheme in investing (though if you find one that works, please let me know), let's actually get to some investing strategy.

I was at the extreme high-end of risk taking, and I got burned for it. Luckily, I realized my mistake before it consumed me. However, being too conservative with savings can be just as dangerous. A recent Bankrate.com survey of 1,001 Americans showed that only 26% of those under 30 owned any stocks at all, retirement accounts or otherwise. In 2014, another Bankrate survey found that 39% of adults aged 18-29 preferred cash over any other investment vehicle. This is a problem, and it's not just because investing money in cash (in itself?) is a paradox.

Cash doesn't work as an investment for the simple reason of inflation: due to economic growth, money earned today is worth less in the future. Have you ever seen those fun cards in tourist shops that say "In 1946, a gallon of milk cost 5 cents," or "In 1971, the average lawyer's salary was $20,000"? That's inflation.

Let's say you have $100 now. If inflation is running at 10% a year, the cost of goods like milk, houses, cars, and candy bars are all increasing 10% per year, all else being equal. As an example, let's say at first you could buy 100 $1 candy bars. Inflation increases the price to $1.10 a year from now, so you can only buy 91. Therefore, your $100 has lost value, even though you haven't technically lost any cash!

Currently, inflation is about 1.5% to 2% annually, which seems like no big deal right? However, even this low inflation rate will reduce $10,000 today to only $8,200 worth of buying power in 10 years. A 4% rate would reduce it to just $6,750.

So, you can see that one needs to reach a return of *at least* the inflation rate just to maintain the starting buying power: keeping all your cash under your mattress effectively burns 2% of it per year. I would guess few people reading this keep cash under their Sertas, but keeping all your savings in a checking account earning 0.1% interest isn't much better. And for those of you who think you scored a great deal by opening a 5-year Certificate of Deposit account earning 1.8%, you're actually just treading water.

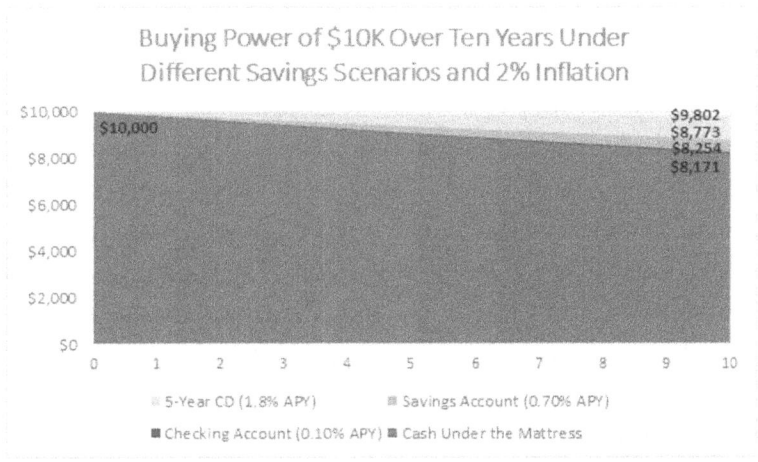

Buying Power of $10K Over Ten Years Under Different Savings Scenarios and 2% Inflation

There are two scenarios in which cash or savings accounts excel. The first scenario is in a deflationary environment, a rarity in modern times. When an economy is experiencing deflation, prices are falling, which means cash grows more and more valuable as it can buy more and more goods. Taking our $100 example again, let's say at first you could buy 100 candy bars, but after candy bar prices deflate from $1 to $0.75, you can buy 150. Sounds great, right? Well it would be, except when deflation has taken hold it usually means the economy is in a death spiral: companies make lower profits, produce fewer goods, and hire fewer people, which means people can buy less, companies make lower profits and produce fewer goods, more people lose their jobs – clearly a vicious cycle. People and companies stop borrowing, and banks will likely implement negative interest rates on bank accounts, meaning keeping money under your mattress actually becomes a good option. The most recent extended period of deflation in the U.S. was none other than The Great Depression (the economy has briefly deflated during financial crises since, but not for an extended period of time).

The second scenario in which cash and savings win out is much more common (and upbeat!): saving for a large near-term purchase, such as a house or graduate school. If your savings are going to be used in one to five years, inflation won't have enough time to chip away at your buying power. Even more importantly, savings and CDs are among the safest investments: they're FDIC insured, meaning you're guaranteed return of your principal (barring a zombie apocalypse). You could possibly achieve a higher return if you invested in the stock market, but if there is a market shock within those five years, you could come out with less money than you put in.

There's one last purpose for which savings accounts are ideal: building your six-month emergency fund. This fund's purpose is to be a resource of last resort, not to earn a high return, so therefore it should be in the safest vehicle available.

The Tax Man Cometh to Help You Retire

When starting your first job, you probably had to review some forms related to your new company's 401K program. Unless you were steeped in personal finance lessons already, you probably also had little concern about it. "Retirement savings? I'm 22 – that's the last thing I'm thinking about!"

If you work for a decent company, you probably also saw that your company would match a certain percentage of your salary based on what you contribute. So, if you contribute 4% of your salary, your employer would match that amount up to a certain percentage. If there's one thing my Dad taught me, it's to never turn down free money, and I think most new employees understand this and contribute the minimum percentage to obtain the company match.

However, this is unfortunately not enough for most workers. With a salary of $50,000, a worker would only be contributing $2,000 per year to his or her 401K under the 4% plan. Granted, that would become $4,000 after the match, but this is still insufficient. Assuming a 5% annual rate of return and 2% annual salary increase, this worker would have just over $600,000 in 40 years, according to Bloomberg's retirement calculator. This seems like a lot, right? It would be, until one accounts for ever-hungry inflation, which at a 2% annual rate reduces this amount to just $272,000 worth of buying power 40 years from now. That might support the average retiree for 10 or 15 years' worth of spending, tops. If you want to see just how much you need to save now to achieve a certain income later on, take a look at Vanguard's income calculator: the results are sobering.

Clearly, younger workers need to be saving more than 4% or 5% of their salaries towards retirement. By most estimates, 10-15% of one's salary is a good target, higher if possible. Due to high spending, many people can't imagine putting 15% of their salaries in funds that can't be accessed for decades without huge penalties, and that's a very understandable concern. Due to the power of compound interest and returns, though, maximizing contributions now can result in much higher sums down the road: the average dollar contributed to a 401K plan during your 20s will be worth $7 at age 65, while each dollar contributed during your 50s will only be worth $1.62 at retirement, assuming 5% annual returns. That benefit is far off in the future and is hard to visualize for those just graduating college. However, there's one other important benefit to 401K contributions that workers can realize *now*.

Ever seen ads for H&R Block or other tax preparers that advertise the huge average tax refunds Americans typically receive? One is inscribed indelibly in my mind. In it, two tax accountants are in a cargo plane tossing wooden pallets stacked with cash out the back. One of them gingerly approaches the threshold of the plane's back door to poke out some last few dollars. Their slogan is "help us return $50 billion of your money back to you, America!" According to the IRS, the average tax refund is about $3,000 per person. Not too shabby.

How did these tax filers get such huge refunds? Well, a tax refund occurs when tax deductions outweigh taxes owed, and two of the major deductions Americans benefit from are the mortgage interest deduction, which we won't cover here, and the retirement fund contribution deduction.

That's right: you may deduct the money you put towards your traditional 401K plan from your gross income, thereby lowering your tax bill.

Let's see how this would affect someone earning $60,000. Under 2015 tax rates, this individual would owe $8,200 for an effective federal tax rate of 13.7%. However, if this individual contributed $10,000 of his income to a Traditional 401K plan, he would only owe $5,720 in taxes, a savings of **$2,500.** If he contributed the maximum allowable $18,000, he'd increase his savings to **$4,000.** That's an annual return of over 20% on money invested!

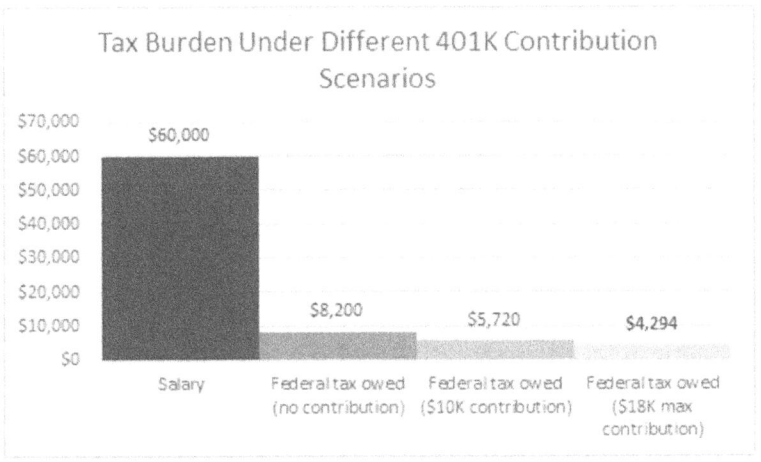

Now, it's true that these savings are only *tax-deferred* and not *tax immune*, meaning that 40 years from now when you retire you will still need to pay taxes on money withdrawn from these funds. However, you'll soon see why this is really not a big deal at all.

So, if you contribute the maximum of $18,000 per year ($1,500 per month) to your traditional 401K plan, you effectively free up thousands of dollars that you can use for other purposes. Some people might use it for a European vacation; others might use it to buy a new car. All of those things are OK – remember, this is money that you otherwise wouldn't have had; plus, you're already saving $18,000 per year for retirement, so why not?

For those who really want to super-charge their retirement, there is still another option available beyond the $18,000 limit towards traditional 401Ks: Roth IRAs. Roth accounts are also tax advantaged but in a different way from traditional 401Ks and IRAs. Unlike traditional accounts, the IRS taxes your initial contributions to a Roth account, meaning that you need to contribute after-tax dollars. However, their benefit is that *any gains these funds achieve are not taxable when withdrawn*. So, if you put in $5,000 in a Roth IRA today, and 40 years from now it's worth $50,000, then you've just made $45,000 *tax free*. Some people look at this and think: Why wouldn't you always do a Roth? Remember, that $5,000 initial investment has already been taxed, so it's less than the equivalent traditional 401K contribution. Earners can contribute a maximum of $5,500 annually to Roth IRA accounts after 401K contributions, making this a perfect use for the $4,000 tax savings mentioned above.

Traditional 401K vs. Roth vs. Brokerage Account: Retirement Value After Taxes

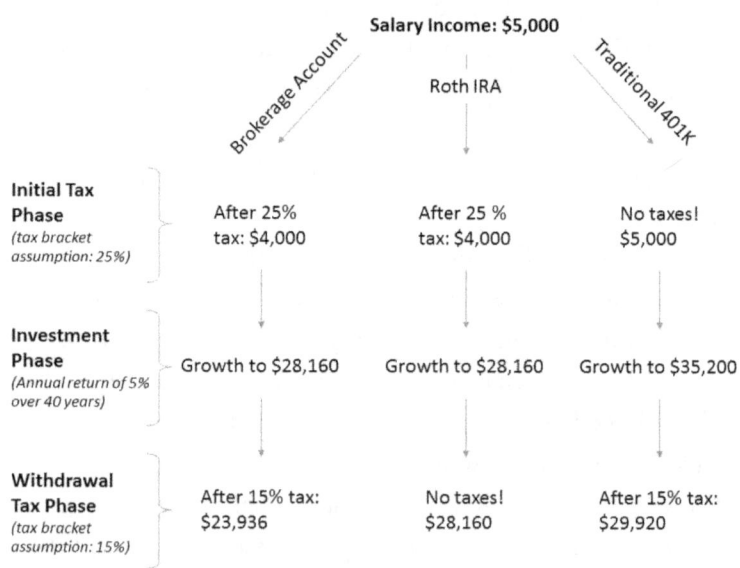

	Brokerage Account	Salary Income: $5,000 Roth IRA	Traditional 401K
Initial Tax Phase *(tax bracket assumption: 25%)*	After 25% tax: $4,000	After 25 % tax: $4,000	No taxes! $5,000
Investment Phase *(Annual return of 5% over 40 years)*	Growth to $28,160	Growth to $28,160	Growth to $35,200
Withdrawal Tax Phase *(tax bracket assumption: 15%)*	After 15% tax: $23,936	No taxes! $28,160	After 15% tax: $29,920

I recommend prospective retirees invest in both their

traditional 401K and Roth IRA, especially if they're young. Why? Fast-forward 40 years for a second (or hop into the nearest Delorean driven by Christopher Lloyd). You've just retired at 65, and you're trying to figure out what your monthly income will look like. You think you can live on $4,000 (in today's dollars, for simplicity) a month. You'll get about $1,200 from Social Security, so you need $2,800 to make up the difference. If you only had traditional 401K accounts, you'd need to pay taxes on all of the $2,800 withdrawn from your account, and who knows what tax rates will be in the future. If you had only Roth accounts, you'd be able to withdraw that money tax free, but you'll probably have less to draw from since your contributions were lower. Well, why not do *both?*

This is a key retirement hack that allows you to take advantage of the graduated income tax, which changes according to your annual income. When you retire, your taxable income becomes $0. In 2015, all of your income up to $9,225 is taxed at a 10% rate; income between $9,225 and $37,450 is taxed at 15%; income earned between $37,450 and $90,750 is taxed at 25%, and so on.

If this retiree just used traditional IRA accounts to fund the $2,800 he needs, he'd owe $381 in tax each month. However, if he drew on his traditional 401K until he reached the $9,225 threshold for the 10% tax bracket, then drew on his tax free Roth funds for his remaining needs, his tax bill would only be $77 each month, a decrease of *80%!*

How does this work? Basically, the IRS only "sees" the $9,225 withdrawn from the traditional IRA account, while the withdrawals from the Roth accounts are effectively "hidden" from the tax man. And that, my friends, is one way to play the retirement game.

Managing Your Money: Less is More

Once you've revved your retirement savings engine into high gear, you can really just set it and forget it if you choose: your monthly contributions will dollar cost average you into the market, so you don't really have to worry about peaks and troughs if you're investing in the broad, general funds. For example, if you're investing a static $1,000 each month, you'll buy fewer shares when prices are high and more shares when prices are low, allowing the shares you purchase when the market is down to appreciate more once it recovers. Just keep your foot on the gas and check your accounts 40 years from now.

However, there are certainly opportunists (me being one of them) for whom the above strategy just doesn't quite sit right. Though you'll certainly be ahead of most Americans if you're contributing the max to your retirement and just buying the broader market, you may miss out on some opportunities. If you're interested in how to increase your returns through slightly higher risk, read on; if not, you can skip to the "Filling the Bucket" section to close out this chapter.

If there's one thing I learned from the economic recession from 2008-2011 and my failures day trading, it's that the most successful investors 1) have a long time horizon and 2) do the *opposite* of what everyone else is doing, especially retail (common) investors. We've already covered the first, so let's now focus on the second.

Quick note: in the following discussion, mentions of "the stock market" and "the market" will refer almost exclusively to low-cost S&P index funds and other international index funds; these observations are not necessarily true for individual stocks or other types on investments.

Baron Rothschild, an 18th century British nobleman and banker, famously said "the time to buy is when there's blood in the streets." In 2012, when the housing market was still stuck in the doldrums with depressed prices, Warren Buffett told CNBC that he'd buy "a couple hundred thousand" single family houses if it was practical for him to do so. The essence of both these quotes is that fortunes are made by going against the grain: buying when the market has crashed and selling when the market is high. Think back to *It's a Wonderful Life*. Everyone focused on George Bailey's heroic self-sacrifice during the bank run on the old Savings and Loan. However, *no one really noticed how Potter made a ridiculous fortune by buying shares of the other town bank for 50 cents on the dollar!* However hateful Potter may have been personally, you have to hand it to him: he was a much better businessman than George Bailey.

In reality, it's very difficult to gauge the top of a market. As Benjamin Graham and Robert Shiller have shown, "Irrational Exuberance" can last for years. This makes deciding when to sell nearly impossible. Moreover, if you have a long-term horizon focused on retirement, you really don't need to sell at all until you're ready to leave the workforce. On the other hand, it's much easier to find a market decline or bottom: prices will have fallen by a lot, and there will be talk in the media of "crash," "recession," etc. As hard as it may be, especially if you've had investments that have tanked along with the market, these are the most opportune times to buy.

Many people think the riskiest time to invest in the stock market is during a fiscal crisis, while the safest time is during a mature bull market run. However, I believe *the opposite* to be true: during a market crash, investors often overreact and sell stocks to the point that they're quite a good value. Further, the more selling that happens, the fewer stockholders there are left to sell further, meaning the chance of a rebound increases.

At the time of this writing, the stock market is quite high by historical standards. However, who knows when the next crash will be. It could be a year from now or ten years from now (I'm betting on the former), and it's truly impossible to tell. So, my current investment strategy is this: 50% of my 401K contributions go into index funds tied to the S&P 500, European stocks, and emerging markets. The other 50% goes into an "opportunity fund" which is in a principal preservation fund that yields only 3%. This opportunity fund is to be used during the next fiscal crisis or market crash, during which I will dollar cost average this fund into the S&P and other index funds that are all but guaranteed to recover at some point. After all, unless capitalism completely collapses as a system, as it almost did in 2008, or deflation sets in, as it did in Japan in the 1990s, the market will recover. Critically, I will also *not sell* any of the investments I have already, due to the aforementioned fact that it's 1) impossible to know when a market is at its peak and 2) impossible to know when a stock index will begin its rebound.

The other investment strategy for the more activist investor is known as the "Gone Fishin' Portfolio." This strategy plays off the inverse price relationships among assets (when stock prices are high, bond prices are generally low, and vice versa) to achieve higher returns than the general market. Diversification is key to this strategy: the creator, Alex Green, recommends determining a set mix of low-cost Vanguard index funds across domestic stocks, international stocks, real estate, and bonds, then rebalancing the portfolio once per year. Rebalancing automatically and objectively sells funds that have done well and reinvests those gains into assets that have done poorly, thereby maintaining the portfolio's overall balance among assets.

While I highly recommend checking out Alex Green's full book, he did post a version of the portfolio using Vanguard funds:

Fund	Allocation
Vanguard Total Stock Market Index	15%
Vanguard Small-Cap Index	15%
Vanguard European Stock Index	10%
Vanguard Pacific Stock Index	10%
Vanguard Emerging Markets Index	10%
Vanguard Short-Term Bond Index	10%
Vanguard High-Yield Corporates Fund	10%
Vanguard Inflation-Protected Securities	10%
Vanguard REIT Index	5%
Vanguard Precious Metals Fund	5%

While the methodology behind the Gone Fishin' Portfolio is sound, I personally have not fully implemented the strategy due to my belief that quantitative easing has inflated the prices of all assets, including both stocks and bonds, so that rebalancing has little benefit at this point. The Gone Fishin' strategy, however, has returned 15.5% annually over the past seven years, handily beating the S&P 500 over the same timeframe, so it's definitely worth considering.

Filling the Bucket: Summary of Investment Strategy for Your 20s

We've thrown around a lot of numbers and terms like 401K, Roth, index fund, and others, so if you aren't already familiar with those terms I can understand if your head is swimming a bit. Therefore, I think it's valuable to summarize the above into an actionable strategy. I know no better way to do that than through an infographic:

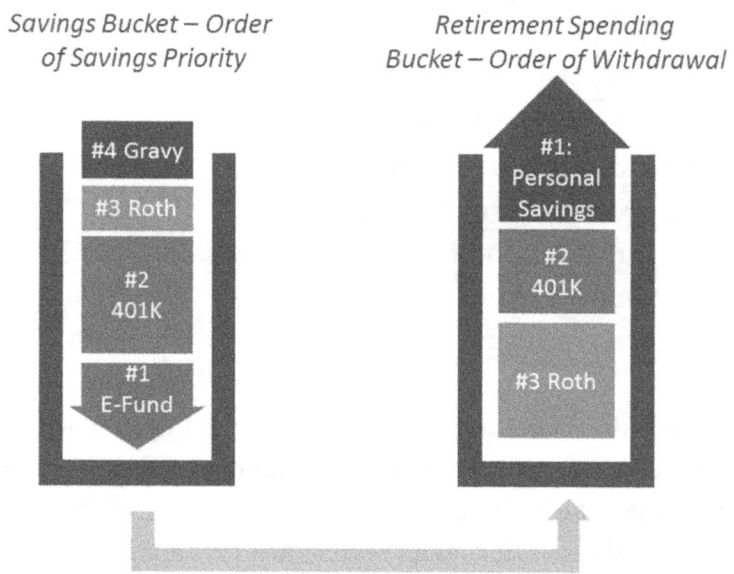

Maximizing Savings Efficiency Now and Retirement Spend Efficiency Later

Savings Bucket – Order of Savings Priority

Retirement Spending Bucket – Order of Withdrawal

#4 Gravy
#3 Roth
#2 401K
#1 E-Fund

#1: Personal Savings
#2 401K
#3 Roth

To summarize: Your first priority when saving should be at least six months' worth of expenses in your emergency fund, invested in a very safe vehicle like savings accounts or CDs. Your next priority is filling the traditional 401K bucket, which your employer hopefully offers, up to the maximum

$18,000 contribution limit. After that comes Roth IRA accounts (contribution limit $5,500) which will give you tax-free income in retirement. Finally comes the gravy: Any extra income saved can go towards a down payment on a house, investment in individual stocks (like Apple) or index funds, or a European vacation, topping off your savings bucket.

In retirement, you spend your savings in the reverse order you put them in. First, spend a reasonable amount of your personal savings (while maintaining your emergency fund), since this money has already been taxed and does not count as income. Next take distributions from your traditional 401K up to the limit of your target tax bracket – probably the upper limit of the 10% or 15% tax bracket for most people. Finally, you can draw from your Roth accounts, whose distributions are tax-free, thereby minimizing your tax bill.

As you can see, investing for the long term involves a lot of trial and error as you find the best model that helps you achieve your financial goals while balancing risk and reward. I hope by now you're a little bit more familiar with the long-term investment vehicles available to you once you become a super saver. Beyond that, I hope you have started to formulate some next steps and action items on how to craft an investment strategy for your future. There's no more important lesson in this chapter than this simple fact: time is of the essence, and a little invested today becomes a lot tomorrow. So go get started.

CHAPTER FOUR

Find a Job You Don't Hate

"Work is so bad; people pay you to do it"

Efficient businesses minimize costs and maximize revenues. We've covered the cost side of this equation in previous chapters – now let's move on to the revenue angle. Unless you've got a big inheritance, your primary source of revenue will be your career.

In aggregate, millennials have had a rough start to the working world. The oldest graduated in the early 2000s and had just gotten their feet in the job door when the recession of 2008-2011 ripped the rug out from under them. Those of us who came of age between 2008 and 2012 looked for work when people with 10 years' experience couldn't find temp jobs. Those who've graduated in the relatively better times of 2013 onward have to deal with stagnant salaries and heavy student loan debts.

Becoming financially secure involves a multipronged approach. First is living a cost-efficient lifestyle; second is learning what to do with the money you save. The third crucial leg of the stool is maximizing your income. Many people ask, "How much income is enough?" The answer to this varies from person to person. However, the more your income increases beyond a certain point, the more you can enjoy its benefits. As it is with good home cooking, income is all about *the leftovers.*

Say, for instance, you earn $30,000 per year. With this salary, you aren't starving, but you can probably afford to put very little away for retirement – much less than the maximum $18,000 per year—and you might struggle to save for an emergency fund. If you get a 10% raise to $33,000, you're not doing much better. However, if your starting salary is higher, say $50,000, then a 10% raise is a little more significant. At $50,000 annually, you can also consider contributing up to the maximum for your 401K and likely have most of your basic living expenses covered. If you're up to $80,000, your disposable income increases even more. $100,000 and above means you can start seriously investing in passive income streams like dividend stocks and rental properties. This is known as the *marginal* value of your income. After you reach the point that all your basic needs are satisfied, the marginal value of each dollar increases as you have more options of what you can do with it.

The reason this book started with reducing costs to increase savings is because this is something *you* control, whereas so much of what can happen in a career is outside your influence. We're now ready to look at the revenue side and figure out ways to maximize your chances of success, and we'll first start with a discussion of career paths.

You Can't Be *Anything*, but You Can Be *Something*

There are three very common yet very dangerous phrases loving parents say to their children growing up. It may sound harsh to challenge these words imbued with parental affection and hope, but they need to be addressed here.

First, "you can be anything you want to be when you grow up." On its surface, this innocuous phrase forges children with a sense of optimism and confidence as they dream of becoming astronauts, famous movie and rock stars, or even President of the United States. It is said with the utmost love by parents, teachers, mentors, and others. The second most dangerous phrase is "you're special." Finally, we have "do what you love and you won't work a day in your life."

So why are these statements dangerous? Let's go through them one by one:

"You can be anything you want to be when you grow up." A common saying is that happiness equals reality minus expectations. The philosophy of limitless career options balloons expectations far beyond the reality of most people and creates a culture of unrealistic exceptionalism. Take becoming an astronaut, for instance. Since 1950, there have been about 500 people who have entered space, out of the roughly billions of people who have lived since 1950. That puts your odds of being an astronaut at about 0.00000001%. Becoming US President is about the same likelihood.

Now, it's obviously important to have dreams, and I'm not saying five year olds should be told they can't be President when they grow up. It becomes a problem if this feeling of exceptionalism continues on into young adulthood for one simple reason: it creates a constant feeling of disappointment, something Christine Hassler, author of *20 Something Manifesto* calls an "Expectation Hangover." According to her book, 80% of millennials report that they aren't where they want to be in their lives. She argues that the *expectation* of success is a major driver of this unhappiness. If you *expect* to become a famous scientist or doctor but don't get accepted into medical school, that is a crushing blow to your life. If you *expect* to become an astronaut but find that you don't meet the physical requirements for flying, it could be equally as devastating.

An alternative is to look at your career as a series of steps. Instead of telling yourself "I'm going to be an astronaut (or judge or musician etc.), chart a course in that general direction and have regular checkpoints during which you ask yourself: "Am I happy with my current trajectory? What do I value now, and how does this differ from when I started this journey? What is the next step for me to advance? Are there any alternative paths that I'd like to explore instead?" This dials down all-or-nothing thinking into an approach that reflects your current situation much more accurately. At each landing point, reassess your position and progress, then determine whether you take the next step on your current path or redirect to a different one altogether.

Furthermore, this simple phrase can create a significant amount of anxiety: if you can be anything and have unlimited options, it becomes much harder to choose a path that feels right. Even if you go down a career path and realize a certain amount of success, you may constantly wonder "what if?" since after all – you could have been anything. This grass-is-always-greener syndrome can very easily slip into disappointment and depression.

People should obviously have dreams and goals. However,

they should be *realistic* dreams with *realistic* goals.

"You're special." As Tyler Durden from *Fight* Club would say, "You are not special. You are not a beautiful and unique snowflake." The problem with "you're special" lies with people who use it as a license to feel superior to others. It's easy to pad your ego by feeling you're both exceptional and the exception to certain rules and limitations. It becomes a problem when people use it as a justification to push forward regardless of objective data that tell them the path will be difficult if not impossible. It often starts in college when high achievers cannot accept the fact that not everyone can get straight A's. A common reaction is to shift blame to the professor, the material, or even one's upbringing. People who feel they're special rarely think they might be at fault.

It becomes an even bigger problem as it persists in your twenties. Thinking you're the exception to broader trends could lead to poor decisions when it comes to investing or making a big financial move like going to grad school or buying a house. It could lead you to underprepare for certain events and challenges because you overestimate your natural abilities. Further, it can magnify disappointments. If you expect to be a standout in whatever you do, it's difficult to pay your dues or stay very long at entry-level jobs, even if you're on a good path.

While it's true everyone is unique and has different skillsets and interests, thinking you're the exception can lead to impractical, half-baked decisions and blame shifting that can cripple your professional development. That's not to say that people can't become special. However, people who reach this point are often the last to realize how special they've become—they've been too busy focusing on whatever it is they're doing to think too hard about their innate worth.

They also realize that the world was not built around meeting their needs—in fact, it's quite the opposite.

"Do what you love, and you won't work a day in your life." If only it was so easy. All we need to do is find a job we love, and we're set for life. However, most people don't even know what work is like until they start it. Especially early in our careers, we have little idea about the variety of professions out there apart from the periodic "Top 50 careers for x year" lists. How then can you "choose" what profession you're meant for?

This mindset is another recipe for a mismatch between expectations and reality. We work hard in school, complete internships, and participate in a litany of extracurricular activities all for the hope that one day we'll be in the job of our dreams; the job we're meant to do.

A lucky few have what they'd describe as "a calling"— usually doctors or other skilled professionals who from early on could not imagine themselves doing anything else. For the rest of us, we're left to navigate the working world to search for that unicorn, and many are left disappointed. We hop from job to job, trying to find something we're "meant" to do. For those who do find what they think is their dream job, they may find that their hobby suddenly becomes drudgery as they're suddenly forced to do it nine to five, every day.

I'd argue that it's less important to think about *what* you do than it is to think about *why* you do it. The primary reason people work is to generate income, and that income should hopefully support your desired lifestyle and long-term goals. It's a means to an end.

So, maybe a career is not so much about finding a job you love as it is about finding one you *don't hate*, as long as it helps you achieve your other life goals. Focus on the environment—the people, pay, work-life balance, and other factors—as opposed to the content. Once you find an environment that suits you, hang onto it. At the end of the day, work is very similar across many fields: answering emails, making spreadsheets, having meetings, etc. are all pretty common parts of a typical day. What's different is the people and culture, and for most people, those are what make the days enjoyable. Though it's never advisable to stay in a job that causes significant anxiety or misery, it's equally dangerous to give up "OK" jobs in the search for that perfect position. Like a unicorn, it may be out there, but odds are good it may not exist at all.

Pursuing Your Passions as Hobbies Outside Your 9-5

While the pragmatism of the above may sound harsh, it establishes the main reason for having a job in the first place, which is to provide income necessary to cover your expenses. People should of course pursue their passions, but it shouldn't be at the expense of earning an income to support yourself.

So how do you then pursue your passions? If you've prioritized finding a work environment that suits you (as opposed to an ideal title or content area), and you're truly passionate about something, then you should have opportunity to pursue that passion outside of your day job.

Maybe your passion is painting. Unlike a day job, painting can be done any time, any place. If this is truly your passion, structure your work life around providing sufficient opportunities to pursue it. Maybe there is an art community you can join, or there could be a gallery or coffee shop where you can display your work. The point is to keep this passion *separate* from your job because the two have very different purposes: your passion provides you happiness and fulfillment, while your job provides you financial security. There's no reason you can't have both.

Eventually, if your passion does evolve into something that could potentially be your own business, and you don't mind doing that as work, you could investigate whether it's feasible to replace your day job. For some passions, that just won't be possible (for instance, I don't ever expect my passion of watching Netflix movies to earn me income to replace my day job), but for some it could be. If it is a possibility, make sure you've evaluated the risks and tradeoffs carefully and developed a rigorous business plan before leaving your primary income-producing position. However, always keep in mind that your work doesn't *have* to be your passion, and it's often possible to still pursue your passion even if it's not in your career.

Why You Get Paid for Work

Have you ever given thought as to why people get paid for jobs? It's not because shareholders want to pay for your rent, health insurance, and date night dinners out of the goodness of their hearts. Workers are paid because they provide *value* in some way.

Firefighters put out fires. Accountants ensure taxes are in order. Factory workers assemble products that are then sold in the market. Doctors apply their highly specialized knowledge to care for the sick.

In all of the above, there's an exchange happening. A firm or government has a need that must be filled, and the worker fulfills that need. The firm must pay to fulfill these needs because no one will do them for free. If people were willing to do the work for free, there'd be no reason to pay anyone. If the demand for that particular need is great and there are relatively few people willing or able to do it, then the firm must pay more to fill that need.

This is the essence of the labor market. To produce goods and services, firms require labor, and for more complex tasks, firms require more advanced skills from those laborers. The reason engineers get paid relatively well is that their skillset is in high demand, and there are relatively few people who have that skillset. It's even truer for doctors and other highly-paid professions. Though jobs like teachers are highly valuable (and some would argue much more valuable than society realizes), the fact is that teachers are paid less because there are many people either qualified or who can become qualified to perform in that role. On the other side of the spectrum, there are professions requiring significant training, such as museum curators and architects, that also have low salaries due to the fact that the demand for those skillsets is much lower.

The discussion I hear around job hunting focuses on "what I'd like to do." There is an assumption that companies are there to meet your wants and desires in addition to giving you a paycheck. If managers do meet those other needs in an effort to keep top talent, then that's great – however, it's not necessarily the employer's obligation. Going back to our discussion about doing what you love, how likely do you think it will be that you'll love a job or task needed by an employer that the employer can't find someone to do for free? Even if there is an employer willing to pay you for that desired job, how likely is it that the demand will be high enough that it will provide a sufficient income so you may achieve your other goals in life like retirement?

Remember that the reason we get paid for work is that we provide value, and it's not up to us how much that value is worth – it's up to society at large. Let's now look at some ways you can increase your worth and therefore your pay.

Find Skills that are in Demand

Knowing that the primary function of your job is to provide income, let's now look at the best means for optimizing that income. The first and most obvious way to do that is by mastering the core competencies expected of your role.

Work is not like school. While good managers will emphasize training and teaching, it is not their primary responsibility to educate workers. If you find skills needed in your position that you currently lack, it's your responsibility to learn them.

Luckily, this is easier to do than ever before thanks to the proliferation of free online education. Organizations like EdX, Coursera, and Khan Academy offer free online courses in skill areas such as accounting, Excel functions, programming, web development, and many others. Courses are often offered in many different content areas as well, such as health care, economics, strategy, and marketing. While "soft" skills like public speaking and professional poise often must be learned on the job, there are often resources online, especially through YouTube, that give you the basics. In this age of information, there is really no excuse for not developing a skill needed for your job, and an effective way to get noticed in your workplace is to become the expert in a particularly-needed skill. Maybe your team has to support sales calls in addition to your regular responsibilities: if this is something particularly valued to your organization, it's a prime opportunity to become the expert in that area. Another example might be use of an IT analytics platform. If it's a core part of your job, and not many other employees are proficient at it, it's a good chance for you to become the expert and raise your profile across your team.

This approach can be applied beyond core job skills as well. In essence, this results in a simple cycle for the workplace: determine the skills your employer needs, learn them, then find opportunities to showcase those skills. Wash, rinse, and repeat.

This should make sense considering our previous discussion on why employers pay employees: employees provide value to employers; employers provide employees paychecks. The more in line an employee's abilities and skills are with the employer's needs, the higher value that employee will be to the employer, which will often lead to advancement for that worker. It's too easy to become reactive in the work place: if my boss gives me a task, I'll do it, but if he doesn't, I won't. This approach will likely avoid your getting fired, but it probably won't result in quick advancement and higher income. If you approach advancement proactively, however, by constantly assessing what skills are in short supply, you stand a much better chance once review time comes around.

Here's an example. Let's say you work at Acme, Inc., a small company that makes furniture. Your job is currently in marketing analytics—figuring out which customers are most likely to buy sofas and recliners so the company can target those customers with advertising. However, you noticed early on that the company's website is extremely lacking and looks like it was made during the days of AOL 3.0. Since you have an interest in web development, on your own time you take some online classes and meet with some friends to build rudimentary web development skills. You take note of why other websites are effective and view your own company's website through that lens. After you've built sufficient knowledge so that you can develop an informed opinion, you could approach your company's webmaster with some thoughts on potential changes as well as suggestions on how to accomplish them.

The above is an example of proactive skills development: determine what skill is needed, learn that skill, and then find opportunities to showcase that skill. This approach could apply to many different areas like public speaking, knowledge of international markets, programming, or graphic design. Now, as mentioned before, this approach needs to be used sparingly—you want to appear proactive but not pushy, and it's always good to avoid stepping on other peoples' toes. However, the more skills you develop, the more valuable you become to the firm, increasing your chances of a raise and decreasing your chances of being laid off.

24

Net worth: $$

Since I was young, I had always dreamed of becoming a history professor. I was a huge fan of Indiana Jones, and I basically learned to read by poring over Civil War history books with battle maps in them. I always excelled in history while in school, so it was only natural that I majored in it. I wrote an honors thesis during my senior year of college and loved the research. I even secured a spot in a summer fellowship program after graduation. Up to that point, all of the above had reinforced my view that "this is what I was meant to do."

However, as I looked further into the future, the picture

grew darker and darker. I read about the difficulties of graduate school and of history PhDs in finding jobs, even if they attended prestigious institutions. I thought about what I wanted out of my twenties, and I wasn't sure more school was right for me until I experienced the working world. I wasn't sure what else I wanted to do, so I decided to take a job with the assumption that I'd figure out my grad school plans in due time.

My first real job out of college was perfect for me: I was a research historian for a small consulting firm. I got to travel to archives and conduct research for a variety of clients. This was what I wanted, or so I thought. After about a year of doing historical research as my full-time job, I became increasingly bored by the work. I was also struggling to support myself on the meager income the job provided. I looked out into the potential path of "Matt Morrill: Historian," and all of a sudden I wasn't excited by what I saw. I needed to reevaluate what I wanted.

Knowing that I enjoyed research and problem solving, I became interested in consulting. I also knew that consulting provided a decent income and some career flexibility, both of which were severely lacking if I pursued history. I applied to many, many companies, and heard back from very few. Despite the dire job market of 2011, I realized I hadn't been focusing on developing the skills employers were looking for—I had been developing the skills I wanted to have instead.

Finally, at long last, I received a job offer from a higher education and health care research and consulting firm. I was somewhat interested in both these areas, but I didn't have a lot of direct experience (other than attending a higher education institution). To my surprise, I was hired as a research associate, which resulted in a 50% increase in salary compared to what I had been earning previously.

Suddenly, I found myself in a career track I would have never thought possible. As I matured with the company, I constantly assessed what skills were in demand. For instance, after noticing there was a dearth of data analysis know-how, I took online classes on my own time to build skills in that area. Another need was knowledge of certain international markets, so I built up my expertise there through research and volunteering for international projects. As a result of this "find-learn-use" skill strategy, I was able to gain promotions and boost my income. Further, the culture and environment of the firm afforded me the opportunity to pursue my passions outside of my 9-5. And I don't have to eat Ramen noodles anymore.

Make the Most of Your Free Time

Though it's hard to believe, your twenties are when you will have the most free time in your life apart from college. For the first time since kindergarten, there are extended periods in which you're not expected to be doing anything – no more homework, no more extracurricular activities, no more summer camps. At the same time, the demands of marriage, kids, and aging parents have not yet hit.

Interestingly, while some people find the forty (or fifty or sixty) hour work week much more intense than college, most of us find ourselves with a lot of free time outside of work. This free time is precious. It allows us time to recharge our batteries, see friends, shop for groceries, and do other necessities. However, it's easy to find yourself with more free time than you know what to do with. If you find yourself in this situation, one option you have is to take on a second job.

We learned from previous chapters how important it is to save money when we're young. Thanks to the miracle of compounding interest, each dollar saved in our twenties can be worth five to seven times that by the end of our careers. If you're living as cost-efficiently as you can, and your primary salary is as maximized as it can be for the time being, getting a second job in your twenties can be a great way to expand your income and build savings even further. You don't want to take on just any job, though. Here are some qualities to look for when considering a moonlighting opportunity:

Flexible Hours. This is probably the most important. Since you'll need to maintain your performance at your primary job, which generates most of your income, your second job should maximize flexibility. This way, you'll still be able to build needed skills and travel as needed for your main job, hopefully boosting your main income over the long run. Flexibility will also allow you to go away for the weekend or do other hobbies while still managing to earn some extra dollars.

Hourly Wage. If it's a side job, it's likely to be paid on an hourly basis. Since your time is valuable, you'll need to find a job that provides a sufficient return on your time investment. You also need to consider the mental energy expended by building skills for a job potentially unrelated to your main career. A job paying just $7 an hour may not be worth your time, especially if that time could be better spent building more lucrative skills. The amount will differ according to each individual, but I'd say a good benchmark is $15-$20: much less than that and the return isn't necessarily worth your investment.

Transferable Skills. While not always possible with hourly positions, in an ideal world your second job would allow you to build marketable skills. Running a website or doing contract data analysis work are good examples of jobs that could help build skills transferable to other settings. Even something like tutoring can build problem solving and public speaking abilities, while bartending could help foster people skills like reading others' body language, which is invaluable in business environments.

Based on the above qualities, here are some side jobs to consider:

- Uber driver
- Blogger
- Tutor
- Bartender
- Pet sitter/dog walker (look into liability insurance first!)
- Yoga instructor

It's far from an exhaustive list, but hopefully it gets you started. While I've had a few moonlighting gigs, the most memorable was the experience I had tutoring, by far the side job I'd most highly recommend.

25

Net worth: $$$

As a result of minimizing costs and boosting my revenue, I developed decent cash flow by the time I was three years out of college. However, I noticed that on the weekends I tended to have too much free time – when I wasn't seeing friends, I'd often plow through entire seasons of TV shows on Netflix or play endless rounds of *Starcraft II*. I'd get to Sunday night, look back at the weekend, and think: *what have I done??*

I'm the type of person who needs to be busy to get things done, so I looked to see what I could do to fill this spare time. I had seen a few job postings for SAT tutoring, and a coworker of mine moonlighted for a company she recommended highly. I thought, "why not?"

I ended up joining a company that offered students individual tutoring sessions. My hourly rate was $40, way higher than my main job. Even better, I had an extremely flexible schedule: though my usual hours were Sunday afternoons, I could modify my appointments as needed, which allowed me to still get away for the weekend from time to time.

Having this second job with a high hourly rate and good flexibility let me substantially increase my monthly cash flow. Furthermore, the type of job I was doing (teaching) was sufficiently different from my day job that I didn't consider it more work, but rather just something different I did with my time.

I found that my mid-twenties were the perfect time to have this weekend gig: I wasn't yet responsible for taking care of kids or maintaining a house. I got to explore a work environment different from my day job, and I had a backup plan in case anything unfortunate happened at either job. What I'm most excited about is the fact that the side cash I earned during this time will have many, many years to grow.

Creating Your Strategic Plan

I'll admit: the beginning of this chapter is at best sobering and at worst discouraging. A dose of reality is sometimes difficult to swallow. However, it doesn't need to be so bitter. I'd argue that creating more realistic, planned out goals and expectations actually contributes more to long-term happiness than having overly-optimistic dreams.

How does one plot a course towards that future? Before

looking towards what the next five or ten years will bring, you must first fully understand yourself and your situation. In business planning, this is known as a SWOT assessment: Strengths, Weaknesses, Opportunities, and Threats, and it is crucial to determining strategy.

SWOT: Used to evaluate new initiatives, people, departments, and really anything else in the business world, SWOT analysis may seem basic at first glance, but it actually gives crucial information that increases the chances of a strategy's success. SWOT can be broken down into two segments: the internal assessment (strengths and weaknesses) and the external assessment (opportunities and threats).

Applied to this context, strengths would be competitive advantages you feel you have, while weaknesses would be skill areas you still need to develop. Opportunities are actions and options you have available to you, while threats are external factors that could derail your plans.

I've given an example of a basic SWOT matrix below, and I'd recommend creating something like this before earnestly embarking on your own strategy development. The exercise is a great addition to Stephen Covey's personal mission statement.

SWOT Analysis

Strengths	Weaknesses
• Data analysis skills • Know about health care • Writing • Teaching ability • Endurance/tenacity in difficult situations • Ability to build relationships • Strong standardized testing ability • Financially frugal/savvy	• Nerves in stressful situations or when presenting to large audiences • "Cold" networking skills • Programming • GMAT score below target • Impatience; "grass is always greener" syndrome • Sometimes trouble finishing what I've started • Don't always make the best use of free time
Opportunities	**Threats**
• Starting a blog or website to write about what I know • Take on more responsibilities to maintain strong trajectory at work • Investigate the potential ROI of grad school • Network with people in my field or recent graduates of programs I'm interested in through LinkedIn	• Prematurely leaving my job for another that does not make me happy • Making a poor financial decision regarding graduate school • Taking on too much responsibility, leading to burn out • Market downturn which could lead to job losses

Myers-Briggs Type Indicator: Another way to conduct an internal assessment is through your Myers-Briggs personality type. Developed by Katherine Cook Briggs and Isabel Briggs Myers in the 1920s, the theory basically holds that people fall into one of sixteen different personality types. These types are defined by four key questions:

1. Are you outwardly or inwardly focused? (Extroverted or Introverted)
2. How do you prefer to take in information? (Sensing or Intuition)
3. How do you prefer to make decisions? (Thinking or Feeling)
4. How do you prefer to live your life? (Judging or Perceiving)

While I won't go into the theory in detail here, it can be a useful indicator to determine what types of jobs or careers might be a good fit for you. The best resource I've found that maps personality type to career choices is Paul Tieger's and Barbara Barron-Tieger's *Do What You Are,* which I recommend highly.

Current State/Future State: The information used from your SWOT analysis basically defines your "current state" – your current situation. It may be helpful to boil this down into a single sentence, such as "I'm a new manager in the field of health care consulting still in the accumulation phase of my earnings career." The next step is to define what your future vision is for yourself.

This task can certainly be daunting and may also remind

Scenario Planning: Current State vs. Future State

Current State: Financial analyst at mid-tier consulting firm with moderate opportunities for advancement		

Future State Scenarios (5 years)	Pros	Cons
Scenario 1: Study on nights and weekends for Chartered Financial Analyst certification; try to get a job on Wall Street	• Likely to result in substantial pay increase • Contribute to financial security • Learn new skills without giving up current job	• CFA certification costs money • No guarantee of success on Wall Street • Terrible work-life balance
Scenario 2: Take the GMAT and apply to business school; seek a job in consulting or a Fortune 500 company	• Attend school again, learn core concepts of business • Potential increase in pay • Opportunity to work at different firms	• Would need to go into significant debt and give up current job • No guarantee it would result in better job • Travel could be challenging
Scenario 3: Continue to pay dues at current company, seek out other ways to make side income	• Benefit from stable employment and longstanding relationships • Pursue side interests with minimal sacrifices	• May become "stuck" with slow advancement • Side income opportunities may not pan out • Could sacrifice long-term earnings by not advancing education

you of corny jokes involving "what's your five year plan?" However, if you want to live your life deliberately, this is a critical step, and it should demand your utmost attention. If you've taken the time to define your personal mission statement, conduct a SWOT analysis, and evaluate your personality type through Myers-Briggs, you should be well equipped for this challenge.

If you have trouble defining a single future state, it's perfectly fine to develop multiple "what if?" scenarios. For instance, you could analyze the pros and cons of a future state in which you attend graduate school versus one in which you join a start-up company. If you're a real nerd, you can even do some financial modeling around each option!

The title of this chapter, "Find a Job You Don't Hate," adequately summarizes its overall message: Your job doesn't have to be your passion, and you can pursue your passion outside your job. In fact, in many ways, it's preferable to do so: when you're pursuing your interest outside of a manager's oversight or customer's demands, you're in control, and you can do what you please. We've also discussed how your job or career is a means to an end: few of us would work if not to earn income, and our income is a crucial tool to accomplish other goals and milestones in our lives. Though not a definitive list, we've also discussed some strategies to maximize that income now so that you're under less pressure to do so later on.

Businesses seek to maximize their revenue and plan for the future, and there's no reason the tools those organizations use cannot be applied to personal finances. What both settings have in common is the need for a *strategic plan* that maps out where we are currently and where we're going. Included in that plan are options and initiatives that help us achieve a desired future state, as well as an assessment of the risks and benefits of various options. In the next chapter, we'll dive deeply into one option in particular: grad school.

CHAPTER FIVE

Think Long and Hard About Grad School

"The only source of knowledge is experience" – *Albert Einstein*

You found a job that you don't hate, and you've been working at the company for a few years. After getting a few raises and a promotion, you seem to be reaching a plateau, with the next advances getting further and further off in the future. Naturally, you look to see what your next step is, and for a lot of people these days, that next step is graduate school.

Graduate school is crucial for certain professions: law, medicine, pharmacy, and college teaching, to name a few. Many grad students derive significant value out of their education, allowing them to advance in their careers upon graduation. Some fortunate workers are able to get their graduate degrees paid for by employers while taking night classes and continuing to earn paychecks. Others are looking to switch career tracks and look at graduate school as a means to that end.

However, at the same time, it's very easy to return to

school for the wrong reasons without fully thinking through the consequences. Obtaining a master's or doctorate is seen as an eventuality, something that everyone *must* do if he or she wants to be successful in this world. Some people yearn to return to the undergraduate life and see grad school as a means to do that. Others feel they can only pursue their true passion if they're studying that content at an elite institution. However, with an average master's degree costing up to $100,000 in tuition alone, this is an expensive way to achieve those aims.

What people often overlook is that graduate school is an *investment,* and every investment's goal is to provide a return. Making a bad decision on graduate school can absolutely cripple your financial future, and too many people take this decision lightly. This chapter is not a diatribe against the higher education industry, and I'm not trying to make the case that no one should ever get a master's degree. Rather, the content in this chapter will help you evaluate the option from strategic, supply and demand, and financial perspectives – in other words, it will help you build a business case on the risks and benefits of further education so you may go into that decision with eyes wide open.

Business Cases 101

Risk is an everyday part of the business world. Too much risk and too little return on an investment can cripple a company, even sometimes resulting in its failure. To help minimize risk when pursuing new ventures, business leaders often must produce a plan that makes the case for a particular investment, appropriately known as a "business case."

Business cases can vary in format, but they nearly all contain three critical components. First is the strategic case for the investment. This includes discussion around how the proposed action is in line with the mission and objectives of the organization. As an example, a hospital investing in a new piece of technology may justify the strategic context of the decision by emphasizing the higher quality of care and enhanced competitiveness that would result. An apartment complex upgrading its units could justify the expense by the fact that it helps the organization meet its mission of providing "luxury style living at an affordable price." Applied to the context of graduate school, the strategic case asks you to identify how advancing your education helps fulfill your goals and aspirations. An aspiring urban planner may answer this by mentioning it's a prerequisite to work in that profession. Someone investigating whether to get a CPA could tie the enhanced education into his or her desire to operate an independent accounting firm someday. This exercise is difficult to do if you have not yet taken the time to create your Personal Mission Statement as described earlier in this book.

The second part of a business case involves the financial case of the proposal. This section requires project leaders to evaluate the costs and benefits related to the action and also look at the long-term return on investment (ROI) potential. Conducting this analysis rigorously minimizes the risk that a firm will make a decision that results in significant financial losses that could destabilize the business. This section will also identify certain key variables that have an oversize impact on potential ROI, meaning they must be tracked carefully.

Third, we have the operational plan. This is the nuts and bolts of how the decision will be implemented. It will often include a list of key action steps, milestones, and other requirements that must be completed. This perspective will include a review of operational risks that might prevent the project from happening.

Though it's not always part of standard business case templates, one last perspective is worth including, especially for graduate school decisions: the market analysis. For decisions involving new product launches, this perspective analyzes the supply and demand for that product and also evaluates potential competitors. We'll see how this applies to graduate school in the next section.

Market Analysis: What is the Demand for Your Degree?

One of the most surprising trends to me in recent years is the continued desire for humanities PhDs despite dire job prospects. It's not difficult to find articles on the humanities job market, and this fact seems to be widely known going in. This is a classic supply and demand problem: there are too many humanities PhDs being produced and too few positions open. The Modern Language Association itself has commented on the dire state of literature PhDs: "Our PhD employment problem is very simply described: there's a mismatch between the number of graduate students earning doctorates each year and the number of tenure-track faculty positions available to them." Why do people still pursue these programs?

Though we can speculate about feelings of exceptionalism ("the job market is bad for everyone else, but it won't be for me") or the mistaken assumption that one's job needs to be one's life passion, I believe many people would have avoided the uphill road to faculty positions if they had first looked at the mismatch in supply and demand.

First is the fact that fewer than 50% of humanities PhDs

are employed at the time of graduation, according to recent studies. An American Historical Association report found that only 51% of students who received history PhDs from 1998 to 2009 were in tenure-track positions. You can also look to books like Andrew Hacker's and Claudia Dreifus's *Higher Education?*, which calculated that universities granted about 100,000 new PhDs from 2005-2009 but only created 16,000 new professorships to employ them during that timeframe. To make matters worse, new graduates unable to find work for a year then face competition from the next classes of graduations, creating a snowball of competition for jobs.

The field of law faces similar problems. Throughout the depths of the recession, law schools continued to churn out new grads to the point that a glut emerged. As an example, in New York, there were 4,771 graduates in 2009 competing for roughly 2,100 annual openings, according to data from emsi. Though the market has improved marginally, there is still a significant oversupply of JDs.

Though you can never guarantee there will be a job available for you at the completion of your graduate studies, there are steps you can take to make that more likely.

Evaluate the Growth Rate for Your Target Degree's Professions: The Bureau of Labor Statistics is the primary source of this information. For instance, we could take a look at the growth rate for nurse practitioners, whose employment is expected to increase by 34% over the next ten years and generate 59,000 job openings during the period.

Calculate Your Potential Competition: To evaluate the number of completions each year, take a look at the Department of Education's National Center for Education Statistics. Admittedly, the database takes a while to get used to, but it's an excellent means to assess the market for a degree. According to recent data, there are about 4,300 new nurse practitioners graduating each year.

Compare Future Supply and Demand: We know that there will be roughly 43,000 new NP grads in the next ten years with about 59,000 new jobs being created, indicating a *shortage of about 16,000 positions* over that time frame. Though of course it's difficult to apply national data to specific regions, odds are pretty good that new NPs will find employment.

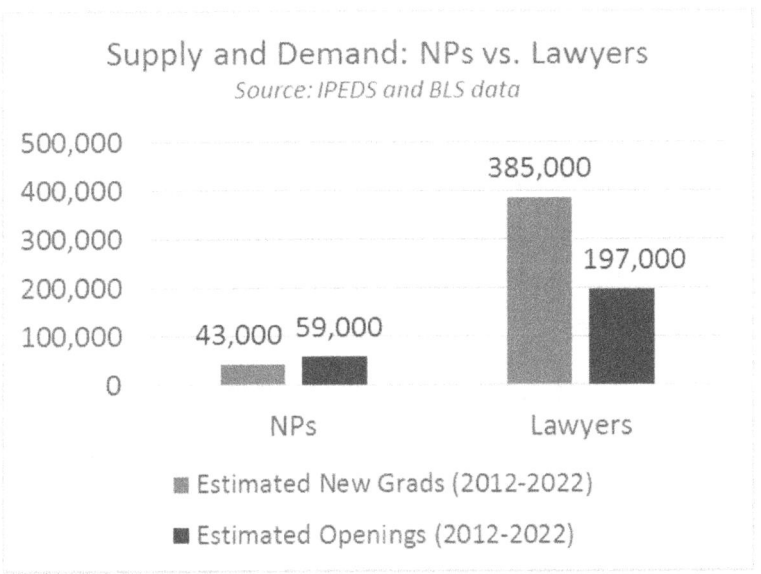

Assessing the market is crucial to maximizing your chances of success. If there are more openings than new graduates in the next few years, odds are pretty good you'll get a job and competitive compensation. Things may work out pretty well if supply and demand are roughly in balance. However, proceed with caution if the supply of new graduates vastly exceeds the expected number of job openings since you'll face an uphill battle in the employment market.

The Cost of Graduate School: Then versus Now

Let's now turn to the financial case. Baby Boomer parents may wistfully recall how they were able to pay their law school tuition with summer jobs. Indeed, though it certainly would have been hard, it was potentially feasible to pay for graduate education with side jobs or by working part-time 30-40 years ago. This is no longer even remotely feasible now. Students often need to take out tens and sometimes hundreds of thousands of dollars in loans to fund their degrees. Further, student loan debt cannot be forgiven in bankruptcy, so it stays with graduates for life until it's paid off. There's talk of a student debt bubble brewing similar to the one in 2003-2007 that rocked the real estate market.

What changed? To be curt: graduate school got way more expensive while average wages stagnated. Let's see how this worked over the past few decades.

By now, you should be familiar with the concept of inflation, which is a rise in prices over time. As workers' wages increase, they can afford more goods, which then allows companies to raise the prices of goods due to higher demand, which then increases their profit margins allowing them to pay workers even higher wages: a virtuous cycle. The period from 1970 to 2000 was one of the most virtuous cycles in history.

In 1970, milk cost 60 cents a gallon, gas was 35 cents, and bread was 25 cents a loaf. Median income was of course much lower too, at just about $8,500 annually. As inflation accelerated in the 1970s and 1980s, the median income increased, so that by 2012 the average household was making about $50,000 per year, an increase of about 660%. However, the prices of goods also increased along with incomes – milk now costs about $3.80 per gallon, an increase of 630%; gas now averages about $2.70, an increase of 770%, and bread averages about $2.99, an increase of 1,200%. So, even though Americans' incomes have increased in *nominal* terms, their *real* purchasing power has stayed about the same and has actually declined a bit in recent years compared to 1970.

Now, let's take a look at how this applies to the graduate school equation, using the example of law school. In 1970, a year of tuition at the University of Pennsylvania's law school cost $2,350 plus a $200 fee. Harvard was a bit cheaper at $2,100 annually. Each school's tuition in 2015 is about $60,000 in 2015, representing increases of 2,550% and 2,880%, respectively, over that time period.

How have lawyers' incomes changed over that time period? The average salary for an entry level attorney in 1970: about $12,000. In 2015, it was $85,000 among private sector lawyers, an increase of about 700%. *The actual cost of law school quadrupled from 1970 to 2015.*

Put another way: a year of law school tuition in 1970 represented about 17.5% of that person's expected first year salary after graduation. In 2015, a year of tuition represented *70% of that person's expected first-year salary.*

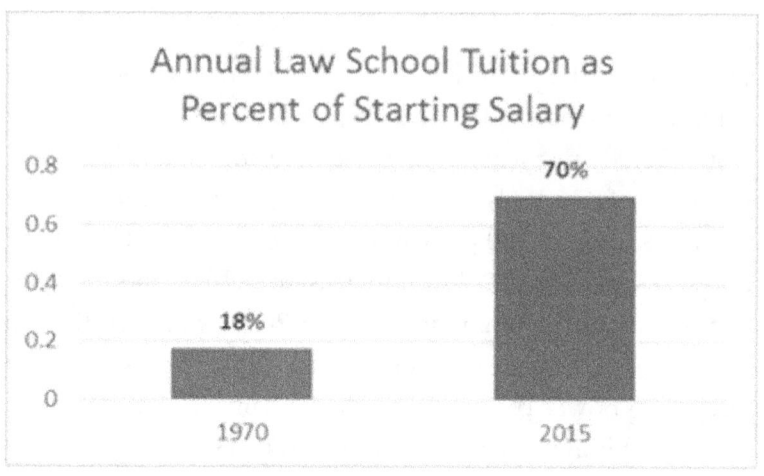

Before you accuse me of being anti-law school, let's turn to more recent history and focus only on master's degrees. According to data from the Bureau of Labor Statistics, median income for a person with a master's degree in 1991 was $55,000, which is the equivalent to $88,000 in 2010 terms. In 2010, the median income for this segment was $91,000, meaning income increased just over 2% in real terms within this timeframe. Let's now look at tuition. In 1991, average tuition for a master's program was $5,100, equal to about $8,100 in 2010 terms. In 2010, average master's degree tuition was actually $14,500, *an 80% increase in real terms over that timeframe.*

When you combine this with the fact that the proportion of the population with master's degrees has increased by 46% over the past 10 years, it's not hard to see why there is a student loan crisis.

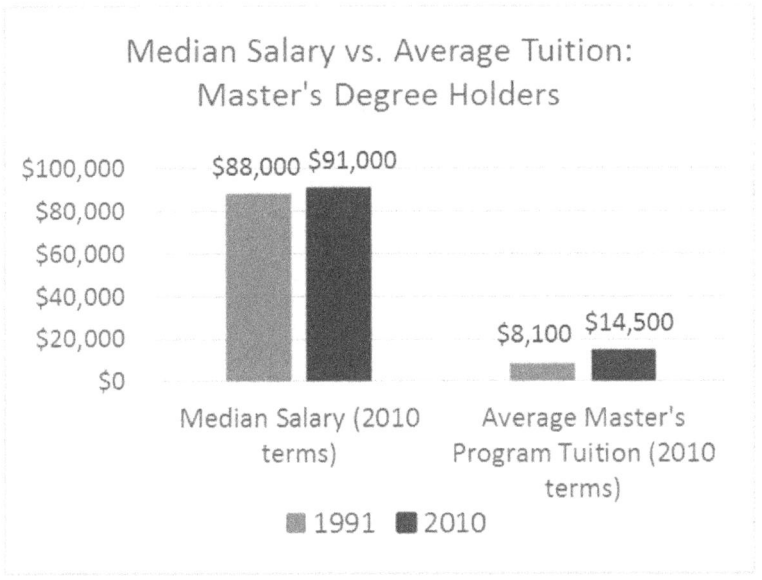

So, what does this all mean? For certain professions, the financial cost of graduate education has substantially increased while the potential payoff has remained stagnant, meaning achieving a return on your investment is much riskier than in the past. Now, you'll always have high-flying lawyers and MBAs who double or triple their earnings by gaining graduate education, but we also have outliers on the other end of the spectrum, such as the law graduate saddled with $350,000 in debt making just $20,000 a year. Such stories are sensational and probably generate a lot of website clicks. However, they're still instructive, and as the above data show, the enhanced financial risk of graduate school requires prospective students to assess the costs and benefits of the decision much more rigorously than ever before.

The Costs of Lost Opportunity

Tuition alone is an intimidating cost to consider, especially once you add in the costs of fees and books. However, there are two other costs that can sometimes be even greater than tuition. Like snakes in a bush, these costs stay hidden and often strike after it's too late to avoid them. As opposed to being directly related to grad school, these costs are related to life as you're currently living it: your current income and your cost of living. Both must be considered to gain a full picture of the grad school equation.

Opportunity Cost: Lost Wages

While such support is rarely available for professional fields, students pursuing PhDs or master's in certain arts and sciences fields often receive free tuition and sometimes a stipend. I often hear this as a justification for attending school: since you're not paying out of pocket for the degree, it must be a great deal.

Not necessarily. Even though the university may not directly be taking funds from your bank account, you're also not putting much into your accounts during those grad school years either. You must consider the loss of the income you'd otherwise be earning as a factor.

Let's take an example. Tim, an aspiring writer, becomes interested in a master of fine arts degree in writing. The program would allow him to work with some leading professors and other writers in his field, but tuition is $45,000 for the two-year program. His current job as an administrative assistant earns $40,000 per year, but the work is unfulfilling. After applying to the program, he is ecstatic to learn that he received a graduate assistantship that would give him free tuition in exchange for serving as a writing tutor. He can get his degree for free!

Actually that degree isn't free. Since he'd otherwise be making $80,000 during those two years, his writing degree really costs $80,000, despite the free tuition. This is an oft-overlooked cost many aspiring graduate students fail to realize.

Cost of Living Adjustment

Costs like rent, food, and other basics play into the equation, but they aren't as significant as lost wages – after all, you'd be paying these costs either way, grad school or not. However, this math changes if your cost of living increases due to grad school.

A good example of this is moving to attend school in a more expensive area such as New York City, Boston, or Los Angeles. Take the difference between your current living costs and add that to your equation. For example, if your current monthly rent is $1,000, but the cheapest place you can find in New York is $1,500, you'll need to add another $6,000 in costs for each year of your graduate studies. The same approach can be applied to food, health insurance, and other necessities.

This cost does work both ways, though. If you go from a high cost of living area to a rural college town with lower prices for essentials, you can credit the difference in your calculations.

Due to the lower cost of graduate degrees twenty or thirty years ago, they used to be a slam dunk financially: you'd be dumb not to get one. However, that calculation has changed as tuition has increased faster than wage growth over the past few decades, making the decision much less of a no-brainer.

The ROI of Graduate Degrees

When business leaders evaluate any opportunity or action, they focus on financial risk and potential return on investment (ROI). For instance, if a business is considering expanding into a new product line, managers need to know that the eventual revenue benefits will outweigh the initial costs of that course of action. This same methodology can be applied to the graduate school question.

First, make a list of all the costs associated with the investment. This should include tuition, lost income, living expenses, and any other direct costs. This might look like the table below:

Item	Cost
Years of graduate school	2
Tuition and Fees	$60,000
Lost After-Tax Income	$55,000
Living Expenses	$30,000
Health Insurance	$2,000
Books	$1,000
Loan Balance Year 1	$100,000
Average Loan Interest Rate	6%
Term of Loan	10
Total Loan Payment	$135,868
Discount Rate	3%

Don't worry about the loan information and discount rate for the moment; we'll get there.

The next step is to take a look at your potential situation after graduation. This requires extensive research: figure out what jobs and careers are available with your chosen degree, then look up salary information through the Bureau of Labor Statistics or Glassdoor.com. Take into account your full compensation, including any bonuses you might get. Next, do some research on how quickly your income may increase in the years after graduation. This is often difficult to determine, since income for certain roles may be relatively stagnant and then jump quickly as promotions occur. Try to take the average annual increase in this case. For example, if your starting salary is $100,000, and it remains relatively flat until you receive a promotion to $150,000 at the end of year 5, then your average rate of increase over those 5 years would be about 8%.

The final part of this analysis will be your existing situation. This part is crucial: we can only count the *incremental* income benefit from going to graduate school as part of the equation. So, if your expected starting salary is $100,000 after graduate school, but your current salary is $80,000, you can only consider the additional $20,000 you'd be getting. In addition to your current salary, tabulate a rough estimate for your living expenses as well.

We'll now determine the timeframe during which to evaluate this investment. For most analyses, a ten-year time horizon is probably sufficient; however, feel free to look at the financial case over 15, 20, or even 30 years, with the understanding that projections get less and less accurate the further into the future we look.

Let's now return for a moment to loan payments and the discount rate. There are many calculators available online that allow you to calculate the total cost of your loan, which includes repayment of the principal and interest owed. In the above example, the initial loan amount was $100,000, which after 6% annual interest over ten years results in a total cost of about $136,000. Annually, this amounts to $13,600 over the time period we're evaluating.

As I mentioned, I was not a finance major, and I expect few of you are interested in the full definition of the discount rate. Suffice to say, the discount rate embodies the time value of money – earning a dollar today is better than earning a dollar tomorrow. It also takes into account the rate of risk-free returns, which for 10-year treasury bonds is about 2-3% annually. It's crucially important when looking at future income.

If this is all getting a little confusing, don't worry – I will be including a downloadable Excel tool as a companion to this book at www.yourroaring20spersonalfinance.com that will automatically do these calculations for you. Using this tool in combination with salary information available through the BLS and glassdoor.com, I was able to plot the projected 10-year ROI of several typical graduate degrees (see the appendix for the full assumptions for each). Take a look:

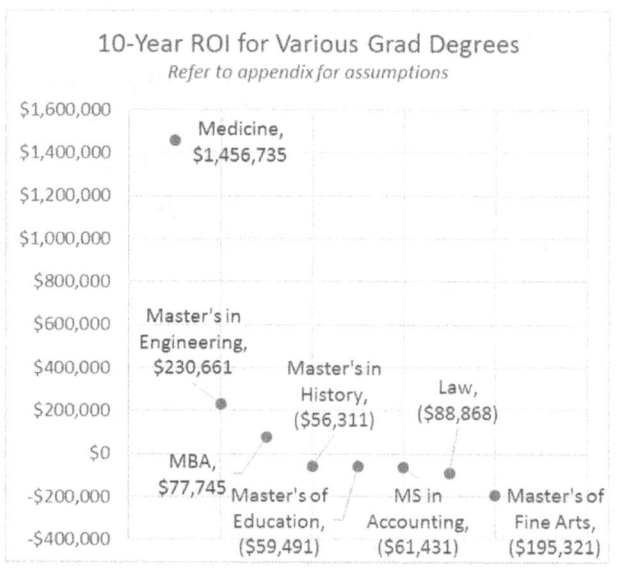

Obviously, there are *many* factors that can affect ROI for a given degree, the biggest being the difference between pre-graduate school salary and post-graduate school salary. For instance, if an engineer was making $65,000 per year before engineering school but $90,000 as a manager afterwards, the ROI would be only $8,000. Similarly, if an aspiring MFA student's prior salary was $30,000 and the MFA raised his or her salary to $60,000, the ROI for that decision would be about $105,000 over ten years.

Financial projections will never give you a 100% accurate accounting of the future – there are just too many variables that could change. What they do allow you to do is compare various options and be aware of the variables that pose the biggest risks and benefits to your overall ROI.

22

Net worth: $

Like many entering undergraduate studies, I didn't know what I wanted to be when I grew up, which is completely fine in college. People come in thinking they'll be pre-med but then take a course in computer science and become programmers. Others are set on being business majors but end up switching to education. As for me, I was always good at studying history, so I majored in it.

I had a fantastic experience as a history major. I was challenged to improve my writing and research skills. I learned to read for comprehension and take proper notes. I also learned how to synthesize content from multiple sources into a cohesive narrative. Further, I was able to explore interests in architecture, political science, and languages (which never did quite take).

In the middle of my junior year I decided to pursue a senior honors project. I planned my research question early, conducted significant amounts of secondary research, and wrote my findings in a 90-page thesis spread across four chapters. I presented my results to my thesis committee and received highest honors.

In the back of my mind, I had always considered becoming a history professor. I fantasized about a life devoted to research and teaching with the clichéd closet full of elbow-patched sports jackets.

However, I was also finishing college against the backdrop of the Great Recession. Millions lost jobs in 2008 and 2009, and employment prospects were bleak for new grads. A friend of mine who graduated in 2008 went straight into law school, despite my pleas to test out the profession as a paralegal first before committing to a $150,000 degree. As I was researching my own job prospects, I came across many articles describing how terrible the job market was for humanities PhDs. Additionally, that path required at minimum another 5-7 years of skating by on a student's budget while my peers advanced their careers. In addition to graduate studies in history, I was also considering urban planning as a potential career path. However, that field was also hard-hit by the recession, and most entry-level jobs required a master's degree. With such dim employment prospects, I worried I'd be unable to pay back the cost of graduate school.

In my last week of college I received a job offer at a small litigation research company in the DC area. I figured I may as well see what the working world is like for a year or two, after which I could return to graduate school, which in my view was a forgone conclusion at that point.

Fast-forward six years. I've found a career in consulting that I enjoy in a field I didn't even consider a possibility as I was graduating. Using some of the strategies I've outlined in this book, I'm much more financially secure than I ever thought possible. I'm now considering whether an MBA is the next step for me.

I sometimes think back on what would have happened if I had pursued that PhD in history, and I don't regret for a second the path I took. The feeling I get when looking back is more akin to dodging a bullet – I would be much less happy now (and in much greater debt) had I gone that route. I attribute my current position to the fact that I assessed the market for each of the graduate school options I was considering, even if I did so in a very rudimentary manner at the time.

Operationalizing Your Plan

You now have some tools to evaluate your graduate school opportunities. While the above are certainly critical to gauging your likelihood of success, the why and the how of the decision are just as important.

As referenced earlier, you need to think carefully about how graduate school fits into your life's strategic plan. If your goal is to study your passion despite forgoing financial security, then you must execute a strategy that aligns with that goal. Similarly, if your goal is to live a comfortable life and provide for a family, then you need to carefully consider how graduate education would help you achieve that – that is your return on investment. If you value getting married early and starting a family, a 5-7 year PhD program that might require you to move often may not be the best choice. The only person who can decide what's best for you is you. However, that does not mean you should blindly pursue your desires without regard to your long term plan. Whatever decision you end up making, do so deliberately and carefully. Hopefully, the tools in this chapter will help in that respect.

If you determine that grad school is the right way for you,

start operationalizing that decision soon. Reach out to graduates of your target program for informational interviews. Determine what standardized tests you need to take, and start studying. Create a timeline for applications that includes your anticipated entrance date. Work backwards from that date and list out all the different milestones you need to hit and tasks you need to accomplish, and start with the first one on your list.

Otherwise, you're just wasting time.

EPILOGUE

Running Your Personal Finances Like a Business

As you've probably picked up by now, if I could summarize this entire book into a single sentence, it would be "run your personal finances like you would a business." Successful businesses do a couple of important things. First, they make sure they have direction and purpose: they figure out what they have to offer and what sets them apart from competitors. Business leaders also learn as much about their target industry as possible so they are properly equipped to enter the market. Businesses optimize their costs and revenues because a business that does not have a positive margin will not be around for long. They look for ways to increase revenues through new products and services, and business owners make sure the products they produce are not what they want to make but rather what the market demands. They try to make the best decisions they can about future investments through rigorous strategic planning and cost-benefit analysis. Sound similar to anything you've read recently?

It's so easy to fall into the norm. Everyone lives in one hip part of the city. Everyone has his or her own place, so I should too. Everyone has a new car; I need one too. Everyone goes out to eat four to five times per week, so should I. I don't need to budget because I earn more than all my friends. This mindset will bring neither financial security nor emotional happiness as every year there will be demand for more and more. When they reach 30, many millennials will likely find themselves looking back on their last eight years, asking themselves: what did I *do* during this time?

I've referenced the term financial independence many times throughout this book. I've also mentioned *choosing* to work rather than *being forced* to work. Here, I'm going to tell you what I mean by this.

According to a commonly accepted rule of thumb called the "four percent rule," it is possible to amass enough savings and investments that the passive income produced by those investments earns enough to cover all your living expenses. The rule gets its name because it refers to the point at which you can withdraw 4% of your savings annually, in perpetuity, without fear of whittling away your principal. The number needed to achieve this is entirely dependent on your expenses. Someone spending $25,000 per year will need $625,000; to support $50,000 per year in spending, you will need a net worth of $1.25 million.

This is my goal. One day, I would like to *choose* to work instead of being *forced* to work. That, to me, is the ultimate freedom. You can see also how formidable a hill it is to climb.

At the time of this writing, I'm at the beginning of my 28th year. As I look out into the remaining years of my twenties and on into my thirties, I'm brimming with optimism. I feel that I've ascended the steepest part of a hill, and while there is still much more elevation to climb, the difficult part is over for the time being. I'm excited that my dream of financial independence is somewhere out there in the distance, and while I can only see it faintly now, it will slowly come more and more into focus.

I don't write this to brag. The fact is, six years ago I started at square one with little money in the bank ("$" to be exact) and a crappy job. There are also other people out there who've been more fortunate than me, as well as a heck of a lot more people who have been less fortunate. Through a combination of (mostly) good decisions, hard work, and luck, one of my goals is potentially within reach at some point in the future. This fact alone should give you hope. If I had made different decisions, like taking on a ton of debt to attend a graduate program I didn't fully think through or allowing my lifestyle to inflate along with my income, my view into the next few years would be very different—I doubt I would have even a foggy glimpse of financial independence on the horizon. I wrote this because these are the things I would've liked to have known as I started my journey into the working world as a twenty-two year old. Though I think I'm approaching thirty from a position of strength, I sometimes shudder to think about how much stronger my position would have been had I started earlier. Even if you've made some financial mistakes or feel like you've gotten off track, there is still time. The power of saving and compound returns is at your fingertips; it only requires motivation and commitment to unlock them.

So: do you want to be starting your 30s (or 40s or 50s) from a position of strength? Do you want, someday, to have the *option* and not the *obligation* to work? It's up to you.

NOTES

Introduction

"Americans Are Not Remotely Financially Ready For
    Retirement." The Huffington Post. Last modified
    November 7, 2014.
    http://www.huffingtonpost.com/2014/11/07/amer
    icans-retirement-savings-
    inadequate_n_6120536.html.
"Buried In Debt, Young People Find Dreams Elusive :
    NPR." NPR.org. Last modified June 30, 2012.
    http://www.npr.org/2012/06/30/155596354/burie
    d-in-debt-young-people-find-dreams-elusive.
"Graduate Of Elite Law School Forced To Live Off Welfare
    Due To Terrible State Of Job Market." Above the
    Law. Last modified October 30, 2014.
    http://abovethelaw.com/2014/10/graduate-of-elite-
    law-school-forced-to-live-off-welfare-due-to-terrible-
    state-of-job-market/.
"Millennials Turn 30: It's Not Us, It's the Economy." NBC
    News. Last modified February 1, 2014.
    http://www.nbcnews.com/feature/in-plain-
    sight/millennials-turn-30-its-not-us-its-economy-
    n11451.

Chapter One

"76% of Americans Are Living Paycheck-to-paycheck - Jun.
    24, 2013." CNNMoney. Last modified June 24, 2013.
    http://money.cnn.com/2013/06/24/pf/emergency-
    savings/.
"The Average 401K Balances by Age." Personal Capital. Last
    modified February 5, 2015.

https://blog.personalcapital.com/retirement-planning/average-401k-balance-age/.

Faw, Larissa. "Why Millennials Are Spending More Than They Earn, And Parents Are Footing The Bill." Forbes. Last modified May 18, 2012. http://www.forbes.com/sites/larissafaw/2012/05/18/why-millennials-are-spending-more-than-they-earn/.

Fleming, John. "Of Americans, 45% Say They're Spending More Than Year Ago." Gallup.com. Last modified August 15, 2014. http://www.gallup.com/poll/174848/americans-say-spending-year-ago.aspx.

Williams, Mantill. "Due to Recent Spike in Gas Prices, Public Transit Riders in 16 Cities See More Than $10,000 Per Year in Savings." American Public Transportation Association. Last modified May 30, 2014. http://www.apta.com/mediacenter/pressreleases/2014/Pages/140530_Travel-Savings.aspx.

"YouGov | America the Intelligent." YouGov: What the World Thinks. Last modified May 11, 2014. https://today.yougov.com/news/2014/05/11/intelligence/.

"Younger Generation Faces a Savings Deficit." WSJ. Last modified November 9, 2014. http://www.wsj.com/articles/savings-turn-negative-for-younger-generation-1415572405.

Chapter Three

"401(k) Savings & Planning Calculator." Bloomberg. Accessed September 7, 2015.

http://www.bloomberg.com/personal-finance/calculators/401k/.

Bell, Claes. "Americans Avoid Investing In Stock Market - Money Pulse | Bankrate.com." Bankrate.com - Compare Mortgage, Refinance, Insurance, CD Rates. Accessed September 7, 2015. http://www.bankrate.com/finance/consumer-index/money-pulse-0415.aspx.

Dogen, Sam. "The Average Tax Refund and What To Do With It | Financial Samurai." Financial Samurai - Honorable Personal Finance. Last modified 2011. http://www.financialsamurai.com/the-average-tax-refund-size/.

Green, Alex. The Gone Fishin' Portfolio. Accessed September 7, 2015. http://www.gonefishinportfolio.com/.

Green, Alex. "The Gone Fishin' Portfolio: The Ultimate Index Fund Portfolio - Investment U." Investment Education & Advice for Investors - Investment U. Accessed September 7, 2015. http://www.investmentu.com/content/detail/gone-fishin-index-fund-portfolio.

Malcolm, Hadley. "For Investing, Millennials Prefer Cash." USA TODAY. Last modified July 7, 2014. http://www.usatoday.com/story/money/personalfinance/2014/07/25/millennials-investing-cash/13152349/.

"Tax Calculator - Estimate Your Tax Liability | Calculators by CalcXML." Financial Calculators from Financial Calculators, Inc Dba CalcXML. Accessed September 7, 2015. https://www.calcxml.com/calculators/federal-income-tax-calculator.

"Vanguard Retirement Income Calculator." Accessed
    September 7, 2015.
    https://retirementplans.vanguard.com/VGApp/pe/
    pubeducation/calculators/RetirementIncomeCalc.jsf

Chapter Five

"Average Graduate and First-professional Tuition and
    Required Fees in Degree-granting Institutions, by
    First-professional Field of Study and Control of
    Institution: 1988-89 Through 2009-10." National
    Center for Education Statistics (NCES) Home Page,
    a Part of the U.S. Department of Education.
    Accessed September 7, 2015.
    https://nces.ed.gov/programs/digest/d10/tables/dt
    10_348.asp.
Campbell, Rhonda. "The Average Starting Salary of Law
    School Students." Work - Chron.com. Last modified
    2011. http://work.chron.com/average-starting-
    salary-law-school-students-7716.html.
"The Disposable Academic." The Economist. Last modified
    December 16, 2010.
    http://www.economist.com/node/17723223.
"Earnings (CPS)." U.S. Bureau of Labor Statistics. Accessed
    September 7, 2015.
    http://www.bls.gov/cps/earnings.htm.
"Educational Attainment CPS Historical Tables - U.S.
    Census Bureau." Census.gov. Accessed
    September 7, 2015.
    http://www.census.gov/hhes/socdemo/education/
    data/cps/historical/.
"Grad Schools' Tuition to Rise To Meet Costs." Harvard
    News | The Harvard Crimson. Last modified March
    3, 1970.

http://www.thecrimson.com/article/1970/3/3/grad
-schools-tuition-to-rise-to/.

Harvey, John. "Student Loan Debt Crisis?" Forbes. Last
modified April 28, 2014.
http://www.forbes.com/sites/johntharvey/2014/04
/28/student-loan-debt-crisis/.

"Income - Table S1. Median Household Income by State:
1969, 1979, 1989, and 1999 - U.S Census Bureau."
Census.gov. Accessed September 7, 2015.
http://www.census.gov/hhes/www/income/data/h
istorical/state/state1.html.

Journal of the America Bar Association, The 57 (October 1971):
1023-1025.
http://www.thecrimson.com/article/1970/3/3/grad
-schools-tuition-to-rise-to/.

Lloyd, Mark F. "Educational Costs (1970-1979), University
of Pennsylvania University Archives." University
Archives and Records Center, University of
Pennsylvania University Archives. Last modified
2003.
http://www.archives.upenn.edu/histy/features/tuiti
on/1970.html.

"Our PhD Employment Problem, Part I | The Trend." The
Trend | The Blog of the MLA Office of Research.
Last modified February 26, 2014.
https://mlaresearch.commons.mla.org/2014/02/26
/our-phd-employment-problem/.

Shin, Laura. "How This Lawyer Ended Up With $350,000 In
Debt And Near Poverty-Level Income." Forbes.
Last modified September 30, 2014.
http://www.forbes.com/sites/laurashin/2014/09/3
0/how-this-lawyer-ended-up-with-350000-in-debt-
and-near-poverty-level-income/.

Weissman, Jordan. "The Unending Horror of the Job
        Market, in One Chart." Slate Magazine. Last
        modified July 14, 2014.
        http://www.slate.com/blogs/moneybox/2014/07/1
        4/humanities_ph_d_employment_the_longstanding
        _horror_of_the_job_market_in.html.
Wood, L Maren, and Robert Townsend. "The Many Careers
        of History PhDs: A Study of Job Outcomes, Spring
        2013." American Historical Association Home Page
        | AHA. Last modified 2013.
        http://www.historians.org/jobs-and-professional-
        development/career-diversity-for-historians/career-
        diversity-resources/the-many-careers-of-history-
        phds.
Wright, Joshua. "Data Spotlight: New Lawyers Glutting the
        Market (Updated)." EMSI | Economic Modeling
        Specialists Intl. Last modified June 22, 2011.
        http://www.economicmodeling.com/2011/06/22/n
        ew-lawyers-glutting-the-market-in-all-but-3-states/.

Appendix: Graduate School Assumptions
Medicine

Existing Situation	
Total Annual Income	$50,000
Living Expenses	$25,000
Expected Average Annual Income Growth	5%
Annual Costs	
Years of graduate school	6
Tuition and Fees	$50,000
Lost After-Tax Income	$40,000
Living Expenses	$30,000
Health Insurance	$2,000
Books	$1,000
Loan Balance Year 1	$200,000
Average Loan Interest Rate	6%
Term of Loan	10
Total Loan Payment	$271,736
Discount Rate	3%
Return	
Year 1 Projected Income	$250,000
Years 1-5 Income Growth Rate	5%

Master's in Engineering

Existing Situation	
Total Annual Income	$65,000
Living Expenses	$25,000
Expected Average Annual Income Growth	5%
Annual Costs	
Years of graduate school	2
Tuition and Fees	$45,000
Lost After-Tax Income	$50,000
Living Expenses	$30,000
Health Insurance	$2,000
Books	$1,000
Loan Balance Year 1	$90,000
Average Loan Interest Rate	6%
Term of Loan	10
Total Loan Payment	$122,281
Discount Rate	3%
Return	
Year 1 Projected Income	$110,000
Years 1-5 Income Growth Rate	5%
Years 5-10 Income Growth Rate	5%

Master's in Accounting

Existing Situation	
Total Annual Income	$68,000
Living Expenses	$25,000
Expected Average Annual Income Growth	5%
Annual Costs	
Years of graduate school	1
Tuition and Fees	$45,000
Lost After-Tax Income	$55,000
Living Expenses	$30,000
Health Insurance	$2,000
Books	$1,000
Loan Balance Year 1	$40,000
Average Loan Interest Rate	6%
Term of Loan	10
Total Loan Payment	$54,347
Discount Rate	3%
Return	
Year 1 Projected Income	$75,000
Years 1-5 Income Growth Rate	5%
Years 5-10 Income Growth Rate	5%

MBA

Total Annual Income	$75,000
Living Expenses	$25,000
Expected Average Annual Income Growth	5%

Annual Costs

Years of graduate school	2
Tuition and Fees	$60,000
Lost After-Tax Income	$55,000
Living Expenses	$30,000
Health Insurance	$2,000
Books	$1,000
Loan Balance Year 1	$100,000
Average Loan Interest Rate	6%
Term of Loan	10
Total Loan Payment	$135,868
Discount Rate	3%

Return

Year 1 Projected Income	$110,000
Years 1-5 Income Growth Rate	5%
Years 5-10 Income Growth Rate	5%

Law

Existing Situation	
Total Annual Income	$50,000
Living Expenses	$25,000
Expected Average Annual Income Growth	5%
Annual Costs	
Years of graduate school	3
Tuition and Fees	$60,000
Lost After-Tax Income	$40,000
Living Expenses	$30,000
Health Insurance	$2,000
Books	$1,000
Loan Balance Year 1	$150,000
Average Loan Interest Rate	6%
Term of Loan	10
Total Loan Payment	$203,802
Discount Rate	3%
Return	
Year 1 Projected Income	$80,000
Years 1-5 Income Growth Rate	5%
Years 5-10 Income Growth Rate	5%

Master's in History

Existing Situation	
Total Annual Income	$35,000
Living Expenses	$25,000
Expected Average Annual Income Growth	5%
Annual Costs	
Years of graduate school	1
Tuition and Fees	$45,000
Lost After-Tax Income	$30,000
Living Expenses	$30,000
Health Insurance	$2,000
Books	$1,000
Loan Balance Year 1	$25,000
Average Loan Interest Rate	6%
Term of Loan	10
Total Loan Payment	$33,967
Discount Rate	3%
Return	
Year 1 Projected Income	$40,000
Years 1-5 Income Growth Rate	5%
Years 5-10 Income Growth Rate	5%

Master's in Education

Existing Situation	
Total Annual Income	$35,000
Living Expenses	$25,000
Expected Average Annual Income Growth	5%
Annual Costs	
Years of graduate school	1
Tuition and Fees	$45,000
Lost After-Tax Income	$30,000
Living Expenses	$30,000
Health Insurance	$2,000
Books	$1,000
Loan Balance Year 1	$45,000
Average Loan Interest Rate	6%
Term of Loan	10
Total Loan Payment	$61,141
Discount Rate	3%
Return	
Year 1 Projected Income	$40,000
Years 1-5 Income Growth Rate	5%
Years 5-10 Income Growth Rate	5%

Master's in Fine Arts

Existing Situation	
Total Annual Income	$35,000
Living Expenses	$25,000
Expected Average Annual Income Growth	5%
Annual Costs	
Years of graduate school	2
Tuition and Fees	$45,000
Lost After-Tax Income	$30,000
Living Expenses	$30,000
Health Insurance	$2,000
Books	$1,000
Loan Balance Year 1	$80,000
Average Loan Interest Rate	6%
Term of Loan	10
Total Loan Payment	$108,694
Discount Rate	3%
Return	
Year 1 Projected Income	$38,000
Years 1-5 Income Growth Rate	5%
Years 5-10 Income Growth Rate	5%

MATT MORRILL